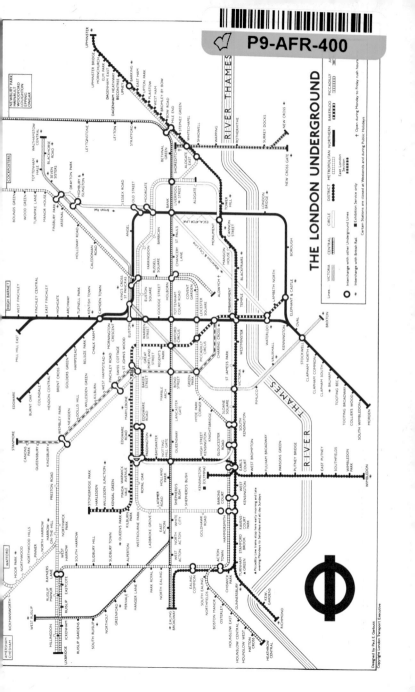

P9-AFR-400

THE LONDON UNDERGROUND

RIVER THAMES

Designed by Paul E. Garbutt
Copyright London Transport Executive

Lines

VICTORIA	CENTRAL	CIRCLE	DISTRICT
METROPOLITAN	NORTHERN	BAKERLOO	PICCADILLY

East London Section

O Interchange with other Underground Lines
✷ Interchange with British Rail
+ Exhibition Service only

† Open from Monday to Friday rush hours
✷ Certain Stations are closed at Weekends and during Public Holidays

A Piccadilly Line trains stop here early morning and late evening Monday to Saturdays and all day Sundays

GOLDEN HART GUIDES

London

SIDGWICK & JACKSON LONDON
in association with Trusthouse Forte

Contents

Text contributions from:
Anthony Edkins, Jean Elgie,
Andrew Franklin, Susan Grossman,
Joyce Rackham, Carey Smith,
Julian Stanley, Paul Strathern,
Paul Watkins, Margaret Willes

Front cover photo: Beefeater
Back cover photo: Parliament Square
Frontispiece: National Gallery
and St Martin-in-the-Fields

Photographs by the British Tourist
Authority, with the exception of
ps. 6, 9 (British Museum/
photo John Freeman

Compiled and designed by Paul Watkins
Editorial assistants: Elizabeth Bunster
Andrew Franklin

First published in Great Britain 1983
by Sidgwick & Jackson in association
with Trusthouse Forte

Copyright ©1983 Paul Watkins

ISBN 0-283-98908-4

Photoset by C Leggett & Son Limited
Mitcham, Surrey
Printed and bound in Great Britain
by Hazell Watson and Viney Limited,
Aylesbury, Bucks
for Sidgwick & Jackson Limited,
1 Tavistock Chambers, Bloomsbury Way,
London WC1A 2SG

Introduction London has been a great city for over 2000 years. The original Roman settlement – covering a square mile on the banks of the Thames – was one of Europe's major trading centres, and nowadays the area of Greater London is more than 620 square miles.

For all its size, England's capital is no amorphous urban sprawl. The 'city of villages' is well named: from sophisticated Mayfair to the winding lanes of Hampstead, each area has its own special character. The imprint of history too, is inescapable. The 'Mother of Parliaments' is the centrepiece of Westminster's palaces of government, and Piccadilly Circus the heart of what was once known as the 'Empire on which the sun never set'. To this day, too, over a third of the world is run according to the theories conceived by a London resident whose tomb stands in Highgate Cemetery: Karl Marx.

London's art treasures are the envy of the world. The Crown Jewels in the Tower of London are unequalled, and the National Gallery houses one of the world's greatest collections of paintings. The British Museum in Bloomsbury preserves the famous Elgin Marbles, from the Acropolis in Athens, and on the Victoria Embankment stands Cleopatra's Needle, an obelisk of pink granite which was erected over 3000 years ago in ancient Egypt.

But London contains more than just history and great works. It is also one of the world's great entertainment capitals, particularly renowned for its music and theatre. It has more resident symphony orchestras than any other city, all performing regularly at such renowned venues as the Royal Festival Hall, the Albert Hall and the Barbican. The ever-changing world of popular music can also be enjoyed, in a range of concerts (there are over 100 every week) featuring everything from Rock to Folk and Jazz. London's theatres offer a similar range, from Shakespeare to Agatha Christie and the latest hit musicals.

All this and much more is described in the following pages. The 'Best of London' features historic buildings, museums and galleries, what to buy and where to buy it, and where to enjoy an evening out. Walking tours and a street plan provide the essential guide to the city's most historic areas.

London

A Brief History

Prehistory In prehistoric times the area which today stretches from London to the mouth of the Thames was thickly wooded and – down by the river – swampy. This prevented any considerable settlement in the lower Thames basin; nevertheless, in the Old Stone Age hunters were roaming this area in search of bison, woolly elephants and wild boar. 8000 years ago, there were small villages to the west of the present city, and the Thames was fished. And 3000 years ago, Neolithic farmers had begun to work the land – archaeological remains have been unearthed at Brentford, Battersea and Heathrow Airport – but the area that was later known as 'The City', located at an unfordable stretch of the river, had not yet been settled.

The Roman invasion In 54 BC, Julius Caesar 'came, saw, conquered' southern Britain. There is reason to believe that he reached the Thames but, before he could make a settlement, he was forced to return to Rome. Almost a century later (43 AD), the Emperor Claudius arrived with an army of 40,000. A permanent headquarters was set up on a small hill north of the Thames, near its tidal limit. A wooden bridge was erected near the site of present-day London Bridge, and Londinium was born.

Peace did not last for long. In 61AD, Queen Boadicea and an army of Britons burnt the city to the ground. Today, the ashes and rubble of this destruction are still being found at archaeological sites 20ft below ground. The city was rapidly rebuilt and it became the capital of the Roman province in place of Colchester. It was eventually (120-200 AD) fortified with a wall, 9ft thick and 15ft high, enclosing three sides of a square (the fourth side was the river) between present-day Blackfriars and the Tower of London. For the next 1500 years the wall determined the shape of London and formed its north and east boundaries.

Connected by its navigable river with foreign ports, Londinium soon became a lively commercial centre with one of the largest forums in the Roman empire, 'a busy emporium for trade and traders', in the words of Tacitus. Slaves, tin, lead and hides were exported; glassware and olive oil were among imported items. Temples were built, including one (dedicated to Mithras) of which interesting remains were only recently discovered. Straight roads, connecting Londinium with Dover (now the A2), York (the A1), and St Albans (the A5 or Watling Street), were constructed. The city continued to prosper until, in the early 5th century, Rome's troubles nearer home led to the recall of its legion .

Dark Ages and Christianity After the departure of the Romans, London fell into decay. The Anglo-Saxons, with their separate kingdoms, seem to have had little liking for cities, and there was no central government or administration at this time. London disappears from historical records for approximately one and a half centuries, until it was adopted by the East Saxons as their capital. This, and the conversion of the

Anglo-Saxons to Christianity led to its revival, and in 604 AD, under the direction of St Augustine, the first St Paul's Cathedral was built. A century later (703 AD), the Venerable Bede was able to note that London was 'a market for peoples coming by land and sea'.

Unwelcome visitors were the seafaring Danes, who sacked the city in 851 and again a few years later. Its fortunes (and its walls and buildings) were restored by King Alfred in 882-3 AD. Another important king in London's history was Edward the Confessor, who, after giving financial support to the rebuilding of an abbey or minster just over a mile upstream from St Paul's, had a palace constructed alongside. The area came to be known as Westminster, and its abbey was consecrated at Christmas, 1065, a few weeks before Edward's death.

The Norman Conquest and the Middle Ages In 1066 William the Conqueror, Duke of Normandy, defeated Harold, the last Saxon king, at Hastings and, following his adversary's precedent, had himself crowned at Westminster Abbey. To consolidate his position he built three fortresses, including the impregnable White Tower (1097) which became the nucleus of the Tower of London.

The first (Lord) Mayor was elected towards the end of the 12th century and, when the Magna Carta was signed in 1215 (confirming not only the Barons' but also the City's privileges), the Lord Mayor of London was the only signatory who was not a peer. Thereafter, the City of London had powers independent of the sovereign and this fact is still recognised on state occasions, when the Monarch presents the sword of state to the Lord Mayor before entering the City. The first detailed description of London (by Fitz-Stephen) is from this time.

London was a major wool exporter to the continent of Europe, and its only bridge was essential to its prosperity. When the Norman wooden bridge burned down, it was replaced by a stone structure. This was in 1176; from then, until its demolition in 1832, London Bridge was one of the city's best known landmarks, with houses, shops, and even a church. In addition to its overseas trading, London was a major producer of every type of goods, including shoes, saddles, girdles and gold. Craftsmen were organised into exclusive associations or Guilds, such as the Fishmongers, the Mercers, the Masons. Most of them had their own livery halls, and the communal Guildhall (built in 1411) was the seat of the City's government. The 92 City livery companies of today are their direct descendants.

The City was dominated by the rebuilt St Paul's, a 14th-century Gothic cathedral; similarly 'two miles from the city, joined to it by a populous suburb' (Fitz-Stephen), Westminster was dominated by its rebuilt Abbey. The great hall of the Royal Palace – Westminster Hall, reconstructed in 1399 after a fire – built as a banqueting-room, also served as the meeting place of the Great Council, the predecessor of both Parliament and the Courts of Justice; it became the regular seat of the former in 1547.

Tudor London The accession of the House of Tudor in 1485 saw London a compact, overcrowded city, beginning to spill outside the old Roman walls. The Strand – the main road from Westminster to the City – ceased to be surrounded by smallholdings and was lined with the palaces of noblemen (Arundel and Somerset) and of bishops (York and Durham). New palaces were built at Greenwich and Richmond by Henry VII; and St James was built by Henry VIII, who also acquired York Place and Hampton Court from Cardinal Wolsey, converting the former into Whitehall Palace. Lands seized from the monasteries, following their dissolution, were used to create Royal Parks for hunting – St James, Greenwich, Richmond and Hyde Park.

On the south bank of the Thmes, Southwark, formerly the site of an abbey, developed into a suburb and became the centre for bear-baiting, prostitution and the theatre (these entertainments were illegal in the puritanical City). The first theatre, *The Globe*, was built here at the end of the 16th century, and in it William Shakespeare acted in most of his own plays at their first performance. Within the City, the founding of the Royal Exchange (1565) by Sir Thomas Gresham made London the commercial centre of the world, supplanting Antwerp.

The Plague and the Fire In the 17th century – and despite the Civil War – the growth of London continued unabated. Between 1605 and 1660, London doubled its population to 500,000, the increase concentrated in the area between Westminster and the City, and in Moorfields. Then, in 1665 and 1666, two calamities struck London: the Great Plague and the Great Fire.

The plague began slowly, but by the summer of 1665, 6000 people were dying each week. Where one person was infected, the entire household would be incarcerated, with a watchman outside to prevent escape; a red cross was painted on the door, with the words 'Lord have mercy' written beneath it. The dead were buried at night in mass graves, without coffins or ceremony, and huge bonfires were continually burnt in the main streets, in the belief that they would keep the disease at bay. One third of the population died. Just as London was recovering from the Plague, another great disaster struck. On Sunday, September 2nd 1666, at a baker's shop in Pudding Lane, a fire started which, over the next four days, ravaged 436 acres of the City. Over 13,000 buildings were destroyed, including the Royal Exchange and St Paul's Cathedral. Medieval London was wiped out and Samuel Pepys described the scene as 'the saddest sight of desolation that I ever saw'.

Rebuilding Immediately after the fire, ambitious plans were put forward for a new, formally-planned city of broad avenues and great vistas, but the City's innate conservatism prevented their fulfilment. Instead, London was rebuilt on its medieval plan, the only modification being the abolition of thatched houses and half-timbering. New houses had to be of brick (or stone for those who could afford it), with tiled roofs. In addition to private building, it was

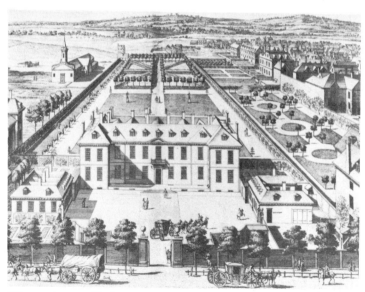

17th-c. predecessor of Burlington House, Piccadilly

necessary to raise public money to replace the City's parish churches. It became the task of one man – Christopher Wren – to carry out this renewal. Wren built a total of 51 churches, designing no less than 17 in one year alone. He was knighted in 1673. His masterpiece, St Paul's Cathedral (completed 1710) took 35 years to build; it dominated the City, its bold dome soaring over every other building. Today, the cathedral and Wren's 23 remaining churches are the City's greatest glory.

While it was being rebuilt, London was also extending in all directions. Many of the major projects were designed by Wren, including the military hospital at Chelsea and the naval hospital at Greenwich, new apartments at Hampton Court Palace, and the reconstruction of Kensington Palace for King William and Queen Mary.

The Squares In the first half of the 1630s, Inigo Jones, commissioned by the 4th Earl of Bedford, laid out Covent Garden piazza, a select residential area. Shortly afterwards, Southampton Square . (today, Bloomsbury Square) was built for the Earl of Southampton, as a setting for his town house. The pattern was followed elsewhere, mainly in the area of London to the west of the City. Here, a few noble families owned great tracts of farmland; with the assistance of agents and builders, they gradually leased plots for building: St James's Square (Lord St Albans, 1665) for example, and Leicester Square (Earl of Leicester, 1670), and Cavendish Square (Earl of Oxford,

1719). These grand squares were originally intended to have a few aristocratic mansions for noblemen but the pressure of a growing population ensured that, instead, terraced houses were built and let to the gentry and 'even to plain Misters'.

The squares were connected by terraces and streets, the names of which identified their owners: Jermyn Street after the family name of Lord St Albans; Bond Street, built by Sir Thomas Bond; Bedford Row – Street, Place, Avenue, Square – all after the Duke of Bedford. The biggest estate of all – the Grosvenor Estate – was the result of the 1677 marriage between Sir Thomas Grosvenor and the 12-year-old heiress, Mary Davies; it covered a large area of what is now Mayfair and Belgravia. Their descendant, the 6th Duke of Westminster, is thought to be the wealthiest person in the country after the sovereign.

The terraces and squares, which make Bloomsbury, Belgravia and Mayfair so desirable now, were all planned and laid out formally, unlike the crowded City. The early buildings were red brick; later, grey brick became fashionable and, later still, stucco painted to look like stone. Although there are important stylistic changes in the Georgian period, the houses are all classical, with large sash windows, elegant cornices, and, perhaps, a porticoed entrance or colonnaded façade.

The last major Georgian development was set in motion by the Prince Regent: having taken over Carlton House (Pall Mall) in 1783 and, with Henry Holland as his architect, enlarged and refurbished it, he – and his next architect, John Nash – devised a plan to connect his House with Marylebone Park, which had recently reverted to the Crown. The result was Regent Street, leading to a newly conceived park and residential quarter, renamed Regent's Park.

Commerce and trade During the 18th century, London's population doubled, reaching one million. To cope with the expansion, new roads were built; and to deal with the increasing traffic, new bridges – the first since the 12th century – were constructed: Westminster Bridge in 1750 and, during the next 60 years, Blackfriars, Southwark and Waterloo Bridges. For the growing trade with the Empire, new docks had become necessary. Until 1800, all goods were unloaded in London Pool (in front of the Custom House) but the congestion led to mass pilfering, and the delays increased costs. New docks were thernore created, starting with the West India Docks (1802), then the Surrey and Commercial (1804), London Docks (1805) and St Katharine's Dock (1828).

By the time Victoria came to the throne in 1837, London was the hub of the Empire. Its warehouses carried goods from all corners of the world, and the colonists were supplied from its docks. The pressure of commerce was pushing people out of the City, and houses were being replaced by offices.

Trains and suburbs With the arrival of the railways, London's growth received an enormous boost. The first line, from Southwark to Greenwich – a four mile track with 878 arches – was built in 1836. The much more important Euston-Birmingham line 'noted for Punctuality, Speed, Smooth Riding, Dustless Tracks and Comfort' opened soon afterwards. By 1850, it was possible to reach most major towns from London, and a ring of main-line railway stations was being built on its perimeter. In the next 20 years, outlying stations were built and London's suburbs were spawned.

Hampstead, Highgate and a few other villages had grown up before the railways, patronised by wealthy people who wanted to escape the congestion and poisonous air of the centre of town. But with the increase of trains and special 'workmen's fares', commuting began in earnest. In 1865, the first underground trains – the Metropolitan Line – ran from Paddington to Aldgate, via the main line stations. Built to reduce the terrible congestion on the streets, the line was an immediate success, and the rest of the underground network followed.

Victorian London In Queen Victoria's reign, London grew more rapidly than ever before, or since; its population increased from two to five million in the 60 years from 1841, growing outwards in every direction. It was a period of enormous wealth – existing side by side with acute poverty. Victorian London saw the rebuilding of the Houses of Parliament and the construction of Tower Bridge, the Law Courts and many museums, theatres, hotels and offices, mostly in the newly fashionable Gothic and Romanesque styles. But, while these splendid monuments were being erected, London's terrible slums, particularly in the East End, were burgeoning. The multiplying population led to gross overcrowding in dark insanitary terraces of back-to-backs, and tenement blocks. This was the invisible side of London that Charles Dickens and Gustave Doré, among others, so vividly described. The energetic efforts of 19th-century philanthropists and reformers partially alleviated the conditions of the poor, but model housing could only be provided for the lucky few, and the last slums were still being pulled down in the post-war years.

The 20th century The beginning of the 20th century saw the continued growth of London, eating into the fields and woods of Kent, Surrey and Essex. By the 1930s, thin ribbons of semi-detached houses stretched 15 miles along the major roads in every direction. This relentless march of suburbia was only halted by the Depression and by the Green Belt Act (1935), which enforced a 'green belt', or a circle of farmland around London, which could not be built upon. Since the 1930s, London has hardly grown, and for the last 20 years its population has been dropping. The major change since 1930 has not been growth but rebuilding.

The Blitz and after During World War II, London was subjected to two concentrated periods of German attack: for eight months in 1940-41, the Luftwaffe battered the capital with high-explosive and incendiary raids; and in 1944-45 it was attacked by flying-bombs (V1) and rockets (V2). London, particularly the dock area and the East End, was devastated. A third of the City was destroyed, including the Guildhall, 19 city churches and 20 livery halls, but St Paul's, the symbol of London's resistance, survived almost unscathed.

Just as a different London arose from the ashes of the Great Fire, a new London has grown from the ruins of its bombardment (indeed, planning for this began during the war, in 1941), and the visual changes have been more rapid and more drastic than ever before. Large parts of London (including the City) are now dominated by skyscrapers and high-rise developments. Two new arts complexes – South Bank and the Barbican – have been constructed; Covent Garden's market has been moved south of the river and the original area has become a centre for small specialist and craft shops, and for restaurants and wine bars; and, deprived of its function by new container-ship ports and tanker terminals as well as by air freight, dockland is in the process of redevelopment.

Today, although London is no longer the capital of an Empire, it is still both one of the largest cities in the world and one of the world's major commercial and banking centres. London is also one of the capitals most popular with tourists, both foreign and indigenous; they visit it, not only for its historic past and for its traditional ceremonies but also because London is still a very exciting and dynamic city.

London Walks

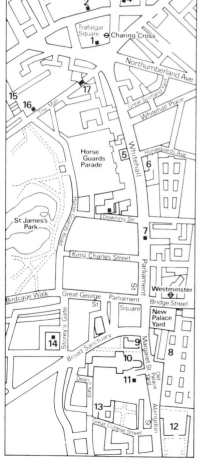

Westminster Walk

This is a walk through an area of heroes and history. Here are the memorials to the men and women who made Britain great, and some of the finest buildings in the land, the great institutions of church and state

Starting point: Charing Cross Tube Station (Trafalgar Square exit).

From here you look out over **Trafalgar Square**, which was laid out in 1829-41 by Sir Charles Barry to commemorate Nelson's great victory over the French fleet off Trafalgar in 1805. In the centre of the square stands **Nelson's Column** (p. 54), a 167ft-high fluted Corinthian column, topped by a 17ft statue of Nelson himself. At the base are the famous Landseer Lions, which were cast in bronze in 1868 from cannon recovered from the wreck of the *Royal George* (a strange choice for a heroic naval monument as this ship capsized ignominiously at Spithead in 1782, drowning 800 men).

Proceed N up the E side of Trafalgar Square past South Africa House, which faces across the square to Canada House opposite. Note the fountains on the N side – whose freezing waters prove irresistible to young revellers during the traditional New Year's Eve celebrations in the square. Cross the road to the pillared Grecian portico of the **National Gallery** (p. 66), which dominates the N side of the square. Here you'll find one of the world's most celebrated collections of fine art, with masterpieces by Goya, Rembrandt, Velázquez, Leonardo da Vinci and almost every other great painter. On leaving the National Gallery turn left and keep left along the railings until you come to the entrance to the **National Portrait Gallery** (p. 67), which houses portraits of a wide range of Britain's great men and women.

Cross the road to the NE corner of Trafalgar Square to see **St Martin-in-the-Fields** (p. 44), an 18th-c. classical church designed by James Gibbs, a disciple of Sir Christopher Wren.

From here continue to the S side of Trafalgar Square. Ahead lies Whitehall, the broad street down which you can see the unmistakable tower of Big Ben. To the right, spanning the entrance to the The Mall, is Admiralty Arch, the terminus of the walk. As you leave Trafalgar Square note the mounted *Statue of Charles I* on your right. This statue dates from the reign of the king, and owes its continued existence to the roguery of a contemporary scrap metal dealer. After Charles I was beheaded the statue was sold by Oliver Cromwell to a certain Mr Rivett. Throughout the period of Cromwell's rule Mr Rivett did a roaring trade selling brass candlesticks, spoons and bodkins advertised as 'souvenirs from the statue'. However, on the return of Charles II he resold the statue in its entirety to the new king.

Leaving Trafalgar Square you enter **Whitehall**, one of London's most famous streets, containing many of the main government ministry buildings. Note *The Silver Cross* pub on your left. This is a favourite watering hole with naval officers from the Admiralty buildings opposite. As it is 'within the verge' of the Palaces of St James and Whitehall, the landlord has to go to Buckingham Palace each time he wishes to renew his licence. (The original licence was granted by Charles I, who allowed the premises to be changed from a licensed gaming house and brothel to a public house.) Continue down Whitehall past the imposing façades of the ministry buildings, and on your right you'll see the **Horse Guards**, built to the designs of William Kent in 1751. The mounted sentries here, in their specially designed stone sentry boxes, hold a special fascination for sightseers. Each day at 11am (10 on Sundays) there is a ceremonial changing of the Guard which lasts for half an hour. The guards are members of the Household Cavalry. Across the street from Horse Guards is the entrance to **Banqueting House** (p. 47), designed by Inigo Jones in the early 17th c., the main surviving

The Houses of Parliament

part of the Palace of Whitehall. It contains the magnificent Banqueting Hall with its ceiling painted by Sir Peter Paul Rubens. It was from here that Charles I stepped out to his execution in 1649.

Continue down Whitehall. In the centre of the road is the statue of the First World War general, *Field-Marshal Earl Haig*, and on the left, the statues of *Sir Walter Raleigh*, (Queen Elizabeth I's favourite who founded Virginia and was the first to bring tobacco to Europe) and *Field-Marshal Viscount Montgomery*, victor of El Alamein. Further on, to the right, is the entrance to **Downing Street**. This surprisingly modest street is the traditional home of the Prime Minister, who lives at No 10, next door to the Chancellor of the Exchequer who lives at No 11. In the centre of Whitehall at this point stands the white stone monolith of *The Cenotaph*, designed by Sir Edwin Lutyens. This was originally erected as a temporary structure in plaster for the first 'Victory March' in 1919, but was later rebuilt in Portland stone. Each year on Armistice Day (a Sunday in early November) a service is held here and wreaths are laid to commemorate servicemen killed in two World Wars and other wars. This is attended by the Queen, the Prime Minister, other political leaders and

representatives of the Commonwealth and the armed services, and culminates in a two-minute silence which is still widely observed throughout the land. The two imposing Italianate Victorian buildings on the right are the Foreign and Commonwealth Office built by Sir George Gilbert Scott (1867) and the New Government Offices which are actually 90 years old.

At the end of Whitehall you come to **Parliament Square**, laid out in the last century by Sir Charles Barry. The square contains statues of several of our greatest Prime Ministers: *Lord Palmerston; Benjamin Disraeli (Earl of Beaconsfield); Sir Robert Peel* and *Sir Winston Churchill.* Disraeli's statue is traditionally adorned with primroses, his favourite flower, on Primrose Day (April 19). Rising high above the square is the imposing clock of **Big Ben**, the nation's timekeeper. Strictly speaking 'Big Ben' is the name of the large bell inside the tower (in fact called St Stephen's Tower), though nowadays the entire structure is known by the name. The tower marks the N end of the **Houses of Parliament** (p. 51), the 'mother of parliaments', where our MPs debate and democratically vote on the bills which (if passed) become the laws of the land.

Opposite the Houses of Parliament at the S end of Parliament Square is

Westminster Abbey (to which the walk returns) and in front of it is **St Margaret's Church** (p. 42). This has been the parish church of the House of Commons since 1614, and remains a fashionable venue for weddings. On leaving St Margaret's turn right. After a short distance is the **Jewel Tower** (p. 52), built as a treasury for the gold and jewels of King Edward III. On leaving the Jewel Tower turn right and through the Old Palace Yard Gardens (on the site of the Norman and medieval palace) and notice Henry Moore's impressive sculpture, *Knife Edge Two Piece.*

Cross Abingdon Street and go into the *Victoria Tower Gardens* to have a look at Auguste Rodin's *Burghers of Calais*, one of his finest sculptures. Then retrace your steps to Great College Street. Go up it and at the end turn right through the archway. This leads you into the quiet grassy enclave of Dean's Yard. The buildings on your right are **Westminster School**, one of Britain's finest public schools. It was founded by Queen Elizabeth I in 1560 and has had many celebrated pupils, including Sir Christopher Wren, John Wesley, the philosopher John Locke, Judge Jeffreys (the 'hanging judge'), and the poets John Dryden and Ben Jonson. At the end of the 18th c. the poet Robert Southey was expelled for objecting to the harsh regime of flogging. The pupils attend daily services in nearby Westminster Abbey, and at coronations it is their exclusive privilege to shout the first 'Vivat!' as soon as the sovereign has been crowned. Leave Dean's Yard by the NW exit (diagonally opposite the one you came in by) and on your right you'll see the famous W Door to **Westminster Abbey** (p. 16) England's premier church, parts of which were built by Edward the Confessor in the 11th c. This building has witnessed the coronations of more kings and queens than any other in the world.

On leaving Westminster Abbey follow Broad Sanctuary to the SW of Parliament Square to **Central Hall**.

This is the headquarters of the Methodist Church. The dome of the Hall has a diameter of 90ft and is the third largest in London (after St Paul's Cathedral and the British Museum). In 1946 this was the first meeting place of the General Assembly of the newly formed United Nations. At the rear of the hall is the *Imperial Collection*, a glittering replica collection of the royal crown jewels of the world, (open Mon-Sat 10-6). On leaving the building turn left up Storey's Gate. At the end cross the road into **St James's Park** (p. 74). Take the pathway which skirts the lake (keeping the water to your left). On the lake there are many different species of birds, including the famous pelicans. Beyond the lake, to the right, is the large open space of *Horse Guards Parade*. This is the venue of the 'Trooping the Colour' by the Guards and the Household Cavalry, which takes place before the Queen on her official birthday (early June).

Continue through the park until you come to **The Mall**. Note the fine view to your left of the *Victoria Memorial* and *Buckingham Palace*. When the flag is flying over the palace it means that the Queen is in residence. The pillared monument at the head of the steps is to the *Duke of York*, second son of George III and commander-in-chief of the British Army (1795-1827). This particular Duke of York was renowned for his insolvency, and it was said that his statue was placed on top of such a high pillar to keep him out of the clutches of his creditors. The magnificent buildings on either side of the monument were designed by John Nash in 1827-32. The entrance to the right at the foot of the steps leads into the ICA (*Institute of Contemporary Arts*) which has frequent modern art exhibitions and also has an excellent cafeteria – an ideal spot for a coffee and a snack. Continue down The Mall away from Buckingham Palace towards **Admiralty Arch**, originally designed as a triumphal arch to Queen Victoria and erected in 1910. Return through the arch to Trafalgar Square.

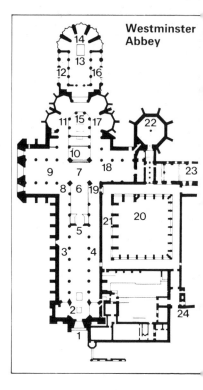

Westminster Abbey

Westminster Abbey Walking Tour

For opening times see p. 45

The original church was built by Edward the Confessor (1042-1065) on the site of a timber church (St Peter-on-Thorny) which stood on what was then an island surrounded by marshland. This old Saxon church belonged to a Benedictine abbey, founded *c*.750 and known as 'Westminster' (or 'west monastery'). The monks believed that a place of worship here had been consecrated by St Peter himself: reason enough for the saintly Edward to direct the building of his own stone-built cruciform church on the site. At the same time the king built himself a palace (the original Palace of Westminster) nearby to supervise the work, thus establishing the traditional residence of England's kings.

The abbey was consecrated in 1065, just before Edward's death: the abbey then became the burial place of the king who had built it. 100 years later, following Edward's canonisation, his remains were transferred to the place of honour behind the high altar where they rest to this day.

In the 13th c. Henry III set about rebuilding the church on a grander scale, in the style of contemporary French Gothic cathedrals. By the time of his death (1272) the building was completed up to the fourth bay of the nave. Like Edward, Henry was buried in the building of his creation, and the tradition of royal burials in the abbey was maintained, with several exceptions, up to the entombment of George II (1760).

In the late 14th c. the remaining part of the Norman nave was demolished and the building completed in the Gothic style. The architect was Henry Yevele, who also built the nave of Canterbury Cathedral. Subsequently, there were only two major additions to the abbey: the Chapel of Henry VII (1519) started by the king himself in place of an earlier Lady Chapel, and the W front, with its twin towers, built in 1734 by Nicholas Hawksmoor from designs by Sir Christopher Wren.

Since William the Conqueror (1066), all kings and queens of England have been crowned in Westminster Abbey. The abbey was the starting place for the pilgrimages to Canterbury Cathedral, and the Chapter House was a medieval meeting place for Parliament. Many of the nation's greatest poets, musicians, politicians, engineers and other brilliant men and women are buried or commemorated in the abbey, which is filled with memorials, statues and plaques.

Following the Reformation the abbey became a collegiate church under the charter granted by Elizabeth I (1560). This means that the church comes under the jurisdiction not of a bishop but of a college consisting of an independent dean and chapter.

The tour begins at the great *W door* (**1**). The interior, looking E, offers one of the great spectacles of Gothic church architecture: a combination of soaring arcades, triforium, clerestory and vault. Interrupting the perspective, at the end of the nave, is the choir screen, itself a rich neo-Gothic masterpiece.

Before the W door is the *Grave of the Unknown Warrior* (**2**), representing more than a million British servicemen who died in the First World War, and memorials to the two British Prime Ministers who were in office during two desperate periods in the nation's history: *David Lloyd George* (First World War) and *Sir Winston Churchill* (Second World War). To the right is *St George's Chapel*, dedicated to those who died in 1914-18: memorial books to civilians killed in the 1939-45 conflict are to the right of the entrance. Here, too, is a memorial to Franklin D. Roosevelt (d. 1945) the only American president commemorated in the abbey, and (on a pillar to the left) the oldest contemporary portrait of an English monarch (Richard II, 1377-99).

The *nave aisles* (**3** & **4**) contain many monuments to famous men, including (centre of N aisle) the unfortunate Spencer Perceval (d. 1812) the only British Prime Minister to be assassinated, and (N aisle, W end) memorial statues to the Labour statesmen Ernest Bevin (d.1951) and Lord Attlee (d.1967).

The ornate choir screen (**5**) at the end of the nave was designed by Edward Blore (1833-34) and contains 18th-c. monuments to Sir Isaac Newton and James, 1st Earl Stanhope. Above it is the organ loft. At this point it is necessary to pay an entrance fee to continue the tour. This leads through the *choir* (**6**), scene of daily services since the 11th c., to the crossing (**7**) in the centre of the abbey, from which the lantern may be viewed – also the fine rose windows of the N and S transepts.

The *N choir aisle* (**8**) is known as the 'Musicians' Aisle', containing the memorials to such great British composers as Henry Purcell (d.1695), Sir Edward Elgar (d.1934) and Sir Benjamin Britten (d.1976). Also commemorated here are the scientist Charles Darwin (d.1882) and the anti-slavery campaigner William Wilberforce (d.1833).

The *N transept* (**9**) 'The Statesmen's Aisle' contains monuments and (beneath the pavement) graves of many renowned British statesmen, including the great Victorian prime ministers Benjamin Disraeli (d.1881) and W. E. Gladstone (d.1898) and earlier politicians such as Charles James Fox (d.1806) and William Pitt the Elder (d.1778) and Younger (d.1806). The E aisle of the transept consists of a combination of three chapels – *St Andrew*, *St Michael* and *St John the Evangelist* – with further monuments.

The *Sanctuary* (**10**) has for many centuries been the setting for the coronation of English sovereigns. On the left of the screen are three medieval tombs (13th-14th-c.) with effigies of their occupants (Earl and Countess of Lancaster, Earl of Pembroke): on the right the 14th-c. sedilia (seats for the clergy) and tomb of Anne of Cleves (d.1557) fourth wife of Henry VIII. The high altar and reredos were made to the design of Sir George Gilbert Scott (1867): behind them is the 15th-c. stone screen separating the sanctuary from St Edward's Chapel.

The *N ambulatory* (**11**) has three chapels, of *Abbot Islip* (d.1532) responsible for the vaulting of the nave; of *St John the Baptist* and *St Paul*; all with 15th-17th-c. tombs and effigies. Up the steps and to the left is the *Elizabeth Chapel* (**12**) which is the N aisle of the larger Henry VII's chapel. Here is the elaborate tomb of Queen Elizabeth I (d.1603) and her Catholic half-sister Mary I (d.1558). Also in this chapel are the tombs of two of James I's children who died in infancy (1606-7); the effigy of the younger child is in its cradle. A

sarcophagus in the same chapel is reputed to contain the remains of Edward V and his brother Richard, Duke of York, the princes murdered in the Tower (1483).

The Chapel of Henry VII (**13**) the abbey's most sublime architectural achievement, has been called 'the most beautiful in all Christendom'. Founded by the king himself for his own tomb, it was completed in 1519 and is the master-work of Robert Vertue. The fan vaulting is without equal in England, and the walls have intricate sculptured detail. Behind the altar is the magnificent tomb of Henry VII (d.1509) and his Queen, Elizabeth of York (d.1503), the work of Pietro Torrigiani of Florence (1512-18). A splendid 16th-c. bronze grill encloses the black marble tomb, which supports the gilt-bronze figures of the king and queen. Below the chapel (now dedicated to the Order of the Bath) are buried the remains of three later monarchs: Edward VI (d.1553), James I (d.1625) and George II (d.1760). (The last-named was the last monarch to be buried in the abbey.) The *Royal Air Force Chapel* (**14**) to the E, dedicated in 1947, has the fine Battle of Britain Memorial Window incorporating the badges of fighter squadrons.

From the Chapel of Henry VII a small bridge is crossed to the *Chantry Chapel of Henry V*, with a tomb of the king, which serves as an entrance to the *Chapel of Edward the Confessor* (**15**). This is the most sacred part of the abbey, containing the *Shrine of Edward the Confessor* (d.1065). Built by Henry III, the shrine was completed in 1269 and became a centre for pilgrimage. On the N side of the chapel is the tomb of Henry III, builder of the abbey, and of his daughter-in-law Eleanor of Castile (d.1290) wife of Edward I. Both tombs have superb gilt-bronze effigies: less impressive is the nearby altar tomb of Edward I (d.1307). Two other Plantagenet kings with tombs in this chapel are Edward III (d.1377) and Richard II (d.1399). Most venerated treasure in the chapel is the ancient

Coronation Chair, made in 1300 to enclose the celebrated Stone of Scone. Legend has it that this was the stone on which Jacob laid his head when he had his dream of the stairway to heaven. In bygone centuries the Kings of the Scots sat on the stone at their coronations, but at the end of the 13th c. it was captured by the English King Edward I and brought to London. Since then the chair has been used for all coronations.

From the Chapel of St Edward the

Westminster Abbey

bridge must be recrossed to enter the *Lady Margaret Chapel* (**16**), the S aisle of the Chapel of Henry VII. This contains a number of fine tombs including that of Mary Queen of Scots (d.1587), erected by her son James I, with the hapless queen in an attitude of prayer. The tomb of Margaret Beaufort, mother of Henry VII (d.1509), is by Torrigiani, with a gilded bronze effigy. Other royals whose remains lie in this aisle are Charles II (d.1685), Mary II (d.1694) and her husband William III (d.1702) and Queen Anne (d.1714).

The *S ambulatory* (**17**) leads back towards the nave, past the chapels of *St Nicholas* and *St Edmund* with tombs and monuments to the nobility of the 13th-18th c.

In the *S transept* (**18**) are the memorials and graves of many men and women of the arts. Most famous is *Poet's Corner*, which contains memorial plaques to many great British poets. The most recent addition is the plaque to the Welsh poet Dylan Thomas (said to have been inserted because President Carter on a state visit asked why there was no mention of his favourite poet).

Proceeding W into the S choir aisle (**19**) the first door on the left leads into the *Cloisters* (**20**), parts of which (NE corner) are 13th-c. To the right is the *Brass Rubbing Centre* (**21**). Straight ahead, to the left, is the entrance to the *Chapter House* (**22**), a beautiful octagonal chamber completed in 1253 and restored by Sir George Gilbert Scott in 1866. From 1352 to 1547 this was one of the meeting places of the House of Commons. Visitors must wear special shoes to avoid damaging the 13th-c. tiled floor, the finest example of such a floor in England. At the SE corner of the Cloisters (next to the *Chapel of the Pyx*) is the *Undercroft Museum* (**23**) with treasures which include waxworks of kings and queens and a replica of the Crown Jewels. The exit at the SW corner of the Cloisters leads into the Dean's Yard (**24**), to complete the abbey walk.

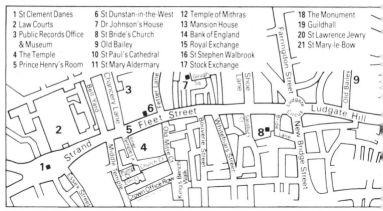

1 St Clement Danes	6 St Dunstan-in-the-West	12 Temple of Mithras	18 The Monument
2 Law Courts	7 Dr Johnson's House	13 Mansion House	19 Guildhall
3 Public Records Office	8 St Bride's Church	14 Bank of England	20 St Lawrence Jewry
& Museum	9 Old Bailey	15 Royal Exchange	21 St Mary-le-Bow
4 The Temple	10 St Paul's Cathedral	16 St Stephen Walbrook	
5 Prince Henry's Room	11 St Mary Aldermary	17 Stock Exchange	

Fleet Street & City Walk

The first part of this walk – through legal London and the newspaper world – follows the route of the Royal Wedding and other important processions, including Jubilees and state funerals. Later on, still in the London of Dr Samuel Johnson and Samuel Pepys, it explores the greatest financial centre in the world

Starting point: Strand

The walk begins with Brotherhood, Education, Courage and Aspiration, the four Virtues who support William Gladstone on his massive statue in the Strand in front of the 'oranges and lemons' church of **St Clement Danes** (p. 41). At the back of the church is the more modest statue of Samuel Johnson who worshipped here.

Samuel Johnson has the best view of the glorious Gothic-style **Law Courts** (Royal Courts of Justice), which contain 59 courts. Opposite is *The George* public house where many legal cases are discussed at opening time, the tiny *Twinings* tea shop and the *Wig and Pen* where law and journalism meet.

In the centre of the road is a pillar topped by a griffin. This marks the site of the *Temple Bar*, the gate to the City of London and the boundary with Westminster. From 1680 a magnificent archway designed by Sir Christopher

Wren stood here, but it was dismantled and moved to Hertfordshire in the last century. On state occasions when the Queen wishes to enter the City she must stop here and hand over the Sword of State to the Lord Mayor before proceeding.

To the N is *Bell Yard* which leads to **Lincoln's Inn** (p. 53) and **Lincoln's Inn Fields** (p. 71). Chancery Lane, on the same side of the street, is famous for its law bookshops and the **Public Records Office & Museum** (p. 68) where the Domesday Book, Magna Carta and other treasures may be seen. On the S side, opposite Chancery Lane, a narrow archway leads into **The Temple** (p. 57). Above the archway is one of the very few houses to have survived the Great Fire of 1666. It contains **Prince Henry's Room** (p. 55) with its Pepys Museum.

On the same side of the street is the *Old Cock Tavern*, which still has sawdust on the stone floor. Beyond it is *El Vino's*, a wine-bar once infamous for its refusal to serve women at the bar but very popular with (male) journalists. On the other side of Fleet Street stands the church of **St Dunstan-in-the-West** (p. 41) which has a contemporary statue of Queen Elizabeth I outside showing her in an elaborate gown and ruff.

There are many narrow streets and

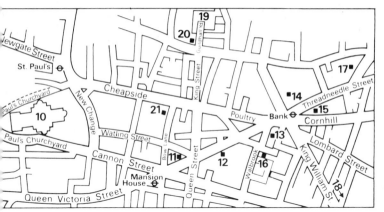

alleys off both sides of Fleet Street and '… if you wish to have a just notion of the magnitude of this city you must not be satisfied with seeing its great streets and squares but must survey the innumerable lanes and courts.' So said Dr Johnson, and signs on the left-hand side of the street direct the visitor to Gough Square and **Dr Johnson's House** (p. 62) where the first English Dictionary was compiled. Down another alley further on (Wine Office Court) is *Ye Old Cheshire Cheese*, one of London's best-known pubs. Frequented by Dr Johnson and many other famous people, it is noted for a delicious traditional pudding which is still served (but no longer containing oysters and larks).

Since Wynkyn de Worde started his printing press 'in Fleetstrete at the signe of the Swane' in 1500, the last part of Fleet Street down to Ludgate Circus has been the centre of journalism. The *Daily Telegraph* and *Daily Express* (with its notable 1930s glass-fronted building) are printed in Fleet Street. *The Sun* and *Daily Mail* are just off it, and many provincial and specialist papers also have their offices in the street. Reuters and the Press Association – the two big news agencies – are both based in Fleet Street.

Just before Ludgate Circus, on the right, is **St Bride's Church** (p. 41) with

its 'wedding cake' spire – Wren's highest and most beautiful. The crypt museum with the excavated walls of seven earlier buildings on the site is of exceptional interest. From Ludgate Circus, Ludgate Hill leads straight up to St Paul's Cathedral. On the left, up Old Bailey, is the Central Criminal Court, the **Old Bailey** (p. 54), topped by its distinctive dome and the figure of Justice. On the N side of the hill is *St Martin Ludgate*, built by Wren after the Great Fire as a visual foil for the vast cathedral. On the S side Ludgate Square and Creed Lane lead to Carter Lane. The medieval street pattern, with its twists and turns, is preserved in this quiet backwater of 18th- and 19th-c. buildings.

After visiting **St Paul's Cathedral** (p. 22) follow St Paul's Churchyard to the right through to Cannon Street. You are now entering the commercial heart of London, with the large new office blocks of multi-national banking and insurance companies all around.

The walk turns up Queen Victoria Street, a main city thoroughfare. On the left at the junction with the Roman Watling Street, is **St Mary Aldermary** (p. 44), a church rebuilt in its original pre-Great Fire Perpendicular style. A little further up on the S side (Temple Court) are the remains of the Roman **Temple of Mithras** (p. 60).

At the end of Queen Victoria Street several major roads run together to create the hub of the City. Here are three major buildings. To the right is the imposing **Mansion House**, the official residence of the Lord Mayor of London. Facing it is the austere **Bank of England** (p. 47), the national bank where the gold reserves are kept in the four floors of underground vaults. Between the Bank and Mansion House is the **Royal Exchange** (p. 56), the third exchange building on the site since its Tudor beginnings. Behind the Mansion House is **St Stephen Walbrook** (p. 45), Wren's 'smaller masterpiece' complete with a small dome that was to be the model for St Paul's Cathedral. The church is now in process of restoration. Dominating Threadneedle Street is the **Stock Exchange** (p. 57) where stocks, shares and securities of companies all over the world are traded on the floor.

From the Bank, King William Street leads down to London Bridge and **The Monument** (p. 53). Built as a memorial to the Great Fire of London, it is 202ft high and from the top there is a commanding view of the Thames, the City and South London.

The walk returns to St Paul's Cathedral from the Bank via Poultry and Cheapside. The *Midland Bank* in Poultry, built by Sir Edwin Lutyens in 1924, should be noted.

King Street leads N from Cheapside to the **Guildhall** (p. 49) from where the City has always been governed by the Aldermen and Court of Common Council of the Corporation of London. The Great Hall and Crypt are spectacular. **St Lawrence Jewry** (p. 42) in Guildhall Square is one of the loveliest Wren churches and is the official church of the Corporation of London. Returning via King Street to Cheapside, turn right. Shortly opposite is **St Mary-le-Bow** (p. 44), another magnificent Wren church. True Londoners or Cockneys must be born within the sound of 'Bow Bells'. From here a short walk takes you back to the precincts of St Paul's Cathedral.

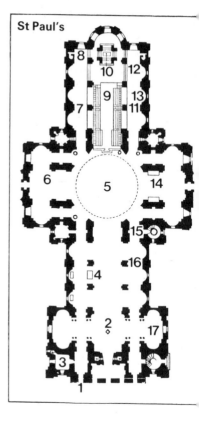

St Paul's

St Paul's Cathedral Walking Tour

For opening times see p. 45

St Paul's Cathedral has always played a very special part in British life. Seat of the Bishop of London, it is the largest cathedral in England and has the second largest dome in the world (after St Peter's in Rome). It has been the scene of many state funerals, including those of Lord Nelson (1805), the Duke of Wellington (1852) and Sir Winston Churchill (1965), and of Royal Jubilees. The Royal Wedding of Prince Charles and Lady Diana Spencer was celebrated here in 1981.

There was a Roman building on the site of St Paul's, but the first church, dedicated to St Paul, dates from 604 AD. Destroyed by fire, this was followed by two further Saxon churches, one destroyed by the Vikings and the other burned down in the 11th c. The church which replaced it was 'Old St Paul's', dedicated in 1240. This massive Gothic building, with a spire rising to 489ft, was more than 100ft taller than the present cathedral. The building was central to the life of the city and the scene of its great events, ranging from the heresy trials of the 14th and 15th c. to splendid state occasions such as the marriage of Arthur Prince of Wales to Catherine of Aragon (later wife of Arthur's younger brother, Henry VIII) in 1501. With the Reformation, the church lost its treasures, and its nave – 'Paul's Walk' – was used as a common thoroughfare for tradesmen and beggars and even for horses and carts. The decay of the building was progressive and in the Civil War it suffered the ultimate desecration of use as a cavalry barracks by the Puritan army. Its final destruction, in the Great Fire of 1666, was a timely fate which enabled Sir Christopher Wren to make a fresh start. His idea of a Baroque cathedral with a dome was at first opposed by the commissioners, but with the support of the king his design was adopted and in 1710 (35 years after the first stone was laid, and still in his lifetime) the building was completed.

During the Second World War the cathedral became the symbol of national unity, miraculously surviving the bombing which destroyed all the surrounding buildings.

The building, in the form of a Latin cross, is dominated by Wren's magnificent dome. Sectional drawings show the ingenuity of its construction: an outer dome of lead on a timber framework concealing a conical supporting dome of brick and beneath this the inner dome with its murals. With its lantern and cross, the dome reaches a total height of 365ft.

The *W front* has a splendid classical double portico, flanked by twin Baroque towers and topped by a pediment with a sculpture of the Conversion of St Paul and a crowning statue of the saint. Entering by the *W door* (**1**) the splendid vista of the nave stretches down to the high altar with its baldacchino. The impressiveness of the Renaissance interior is related not only to its length (463ft) but to its width (at 125ft, the widest Anglican nave in England). It seats 2500 for services and recitals.

In the centre of the floor at the W end of the nave is the *Night Watch Memorial Stone* (**2**), commemorating the intrepid fire-fighters who saved the cathedral from destruction in the last war. In the NW corner of the cathedral is *All Soul's Chapel* (**3**) with a memorial to Lord Kitchener (d.1916) and to soldiers of the First World War. Proceeding up the *N aisle*, the colossal monument (**4**) to the Duke of Wellington (d.1852) is seen under the third arch of the nave arcade.

At the crossing (**5**) the cathedral's great inner *dome* rises 218ft above the floor. It is decorated with eight murals of the Life of St Paul, by Sir James Thornhill (1715-21). Below the windows in the drum of the dome is the *Whispering Gallery*, remarkable for its acoustics. The spandrels of the arches supporting the dome are decorated with mosaics of the Evangelists and Prophets: the quarter domes below the arches have mosaics of the Crucifixion, Entombment, Resurrection and Ascension.

The *N transept* (**6**), badly damaged by a bomb in 1941, has a fine classical font by Francis Bird (1727). The *N choir aisle* or *ambulatory* (**7**) is entered by wrought-iron gates designed by the Frenchman Jean Tijou who worked in the cathedral 1691-1709. The aisle contains an exhibition of photographs of the recent Royal Wedding. At the E end is the *Chapel of Modern Martyrs* (**8**) commemorating Anglican martyrs since 1850.

The *Choir* (**9**) is entered through the

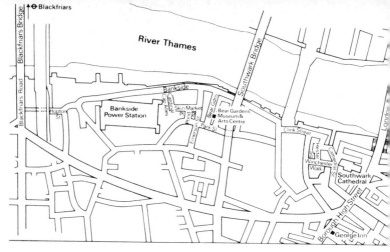

Tijou Gates (early 18th-c.) one of the finest examples of wrought-iron work in the world. The choir stalls and organ case are decorated with wood-carvings by Grinling Gibbons (1690s). His autograph – an open pea-pod – may be seen in a number of carvings. The ceiling mosaics in the choir are by Sir William Richmond (1891-1904) and represent the Creation of the Beasts, Birds and Fishes. The High Altar (**10**) with its baldacchino or canopy are a modern copy of Wren's originals, destroyed by a bomb, and a memorial to the Commonwealth dead of both World Wars. The *American Memorial Chapel* behind the High Altar is a British tribute to the 28,000 US servicemen based in Britain who lost their lives in the last war. American flowers are shown in the carvings, and the stained glass depicts the emblem of each state in the Union.

The *S choir aisle* (**11**) contains the Lady Chapel (**12**) and a *Memorial to John Donne* (**13**), the only monument to survive the Great Fire intact. The poet Donne (d.1631) was Dean of St Paul's.

From the *S transept* (**14**) a staircase leads down to the **Crypt**. Said to be the largest in Europe, the crypt is one of the most fascinating parts of the cathedral. Wren is buried here with the inscription (in Latin) 'If you seek his monument, look around you'. Others with memorials in the 'Artist's Corner' include William Blake, J. M. W. Turner, Sir Joshua Reynolds, Sir John Everett Millais and John Singer Sargent. The tombs of the Duke of Wellington and Lord Nelson are also here, along with memorials to numerous other military leaders. The crypt contains the *O.B.E. Chapel* (dedicated 1960), an exhibition of the cathedral treasures and a fascinating model by Sir Christopher Wren of an earlier design for the cathedral.

The entrance to the *Whispering Gallery* (**15**) is from a doorway in the *S aisle*. The gallery, 100ft above the floor of the cathedral, owes its name to the fact that voices whispered against the wall on one side can be heard near the wall on the opposite side. From here you can also reach the *Stone Gallery* at the base of the outer dome and the *Golden Gallery* (399 steps) at the foot of the lantern, which offer commanding views of London. Further along in the S aisle is the famous painting *The Light of the World* (**16**) by W. Holman Hunt (1900), an autograph version of the original in Keble College, Oxford.

The *Chapel of St Michael and St George* (**17**) is beneath the W clock tower and commemorates members of that distinguished Order.

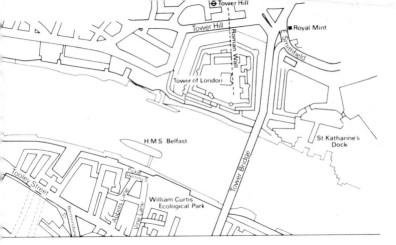

River Walk

This walk takes you along the banks of the Thames and through the heart of Shakespearean Southwark, with views of the Pool of London, the City skyline and the river's most famous bridges

Starting point: Blackfriars Tube Station Have a look (and a pint?) at the triangular *Black Friars* pub on the opposite side of the road from the station. It is remarkable for its copper and marble wall decorations inside, and is perhaps the finest example of Art-Deco craftsmanship in London. Then head S towards **Blackfriars Bridge**. Note the underpass just before you reach the bridge. During the recent excavations for this roadway the wooden frame of a Roman ship was discovered. This riverside site was part of the ancient Roman port of Londinium. Blackfriars Bridge is named after a Dominican Priory (home of the celebrated Black Friars) which once stood near this spot. There's a culvert beneath the bridge – this is the mouth of the *River Fleet*, one of London's 'hidden' rivers, which flows beneath nearby Fleet Street. As you cross Blackfriars Bridge, to your right you see the skyline of London's West End and the line of historic ships permanently moored along the Victoria Embankment.

At the end of Blackfriars Bridge take the first turn to the left down the footpath with the black and white bollards. After passing under the Blackfriars Railway Bridge, turn left and keep going along the modern **Bankside** waterfront towards *The Founder's Arms* pub – a popular spot for a summer evening pint with its views of the city across the river. Past the pub to the right is the monolithic structure of the *Bankside Power Station*. From Bankside one has the best views of the city. Note the towering dome of *St Paul's Cathedral*, with the red-brick *College of Arms* in front where the Royal Heralds have their offices. Behind St Paul's are the jagged towers of the *Barbican*, while to the right is England's tallest building, the *National Westminster Tower*.

During the 18th c. the Thames flowed more slowly at this point and in winter it would sometimes freeze over. This was the site of the famous Ice Fairs, when booths, fairgrounds and all kinds of stalls would be set up on the ice. At the end of the last Ice Fair in 1810 the thaw set in so quickly that many of the booths were carried off downstream. With the removal of old London Bridge (which acted as a partial dam) and the construction of the Embankments which narrowed the river, the rise and fall of the tide

Tower Bridge

increased and the river began to flow more quickly here, thus preventing it from freezing over.

Just past Bankside Power Station you come to a row of restored 18th-c. buildings which show what the old Bankside was like. Note the plaque on *No 49, Cardinal Wharf*: this was where Sir Christopher Wren watched the building of St Paul's Cathedral (1675-1710) across the river. Beside No 49 is the narrow entrance to Cardinal Cap Alley. Continue down this alley and then left into Skin Market Place. On the vacant plot of land to your left there are ambitious plans to build a full-scale reproduction of the Globe Theatre. The exact location of

Shakespeare's Globe (where he acted, was a shareholder and most of his plays were first performed) is not known, but it might have been this site. This is the heart of ancient **Southwark**, which in the 16th and 17th c. was London's Soho-style entertainment district. There were numerous theatres, bear-baiting rings, taverns and brothels. The brothels or 'stews' as they were known, where the prostitutes were famous for going about bare-breasted, were all on land owned by the Bishop of Winchester.

From Skin Market Place turn right into Emerson Street, left into Park Street and first left into Bear Gardens. Here on the right is the **Bear Gardens Museum** (p. 61) which contains an Elizabethan Theatre exhibition. From the museum continue down Bear Gardens towards the river. Here turn right along the embankment. Pass under Southwark Bridge and follow the boarded walk which leads through the building site back to the riverside. On the corner by Cannon Street Railway Bridge you'll see *The Anchor* pub. This is one of the original Bankside taverns. Most of the present building is 18th-c., though timbers from the earlier structure remain. Dr Samuel Johnson is said to have been general manager here, and his memory is still commemorated on the traditional bill of fare in the form of 'Dr Johnson's Veal'. Turn right at *The Anchor*, and then first left under Cannon Street Bridge into **Clink Street**. This was once the site of the notorious Clink Prison, where many a Southwark reveller spent the night 'in the clink'. As you enter Clink Street there is a plaque on the wall to the left which gives details of some of the prison's more celebrated inmates. Continue down the narrow confines of this street, between the high Victorian warehouses, and do not miss, on the right, the excavated remains of the 14th-c. *Bishop of Winchester's Palace*. The impressive rose window is particularly surprising in this otherwise rather derelict area. At the end of Clink Street turn right, and then take the second left down Winchester Walk. At the end of this short street you'll see **Southwark Cathedral** (p. 45), one of London's most impressive Gothic churches. Continue straight across Cathedral Street into the cathedral precinct, and enter the cathedral by the door to your left.

On leaving the cathedral turn left and continue through the cathedral precinct which leads up some steps into Borough High Street. Here make a short detour up Borough High Street away from the river to *The George* tavern. Well known to Shakespeare and Charles Dickens (who mentions it in *Little Dorrit*), it is the last remaining galleried inn in London. It still serves good beer and has a pleasant restaurant on the first floor. Retrace your steps towards **London Bridge**. Recent archeological evidence has shown that there has been a bridge across the Thames at this point since Roman times, and until 1750 London Bridge was the only bridge across the river. The ancient bridge carried houses and shops, and at each end there was a fortified gate with spikes. By tradition the executed heads of traitors were placed on these spikes. The ancient bridge was finally demolished in 1832, and a new one was built by John Rennie. The present bridge was completed in 1972, and John Rennie's bridge was transported stone by stone to be re-erected at Lake Havasu in Arizona. Just before the bridge and in front of the classical Hibernia Chambers, take the steps down, go under the bridge and E along Tooley Street. Shortly on the right is the *London Dungeon* (p. 77), containing many gruesome exhibits from the capital's past. This museum is not suitable for young children or the faint-hearted.

Continue down Tooley Street to Abbots Lane on the left. This leads to Pickle Herring Street. Follow the signs for **HMS Belfast** (p. 64) onto the river front where the ship is moored. This was once the largest cruiser in the

Royal Navy and is now a fascinating floating naval museum.

If you wish to cut the walk short – in summer only – there is a ferry across the river to the Tower of London. Otherwise, on leaving the *HMS Belfast*, continue E along the riverside towards Tower Bridge. On your right you'll see the *William Curtis Ecological Park* at Potters Fields. (The main entrance is around the corner in Vine Lane, a continuation of Pickle Herring Street). This park was established in 1977 as an urban nature reserve. It contains all kinds of plants and grasses which can be found in and around London, as well as many species which are being grown experimentally with the aim of introducing them to the capital. The stretch of river here is known as **The Pool of London**. Nowadays the main port of London is several miles downstream at Tilbury, but until the 1930s the Pool was the busiest stretch of the Thames. At the end of the last century the congestion was so great that it was sometimes possible to walk from one bank of the river to the other across the decks of the docked ships and unloading barges.

Continue along the riverside walk to **Tower Bridge**. This part-suspension, part-drawbridge was opened in 1894 and is now one of London's most familiar sights. Nowadays the drawbridge is seldom opened, except to allow visiting tall-ships into the Pool of London. Visit the museum under the bridge, where there is an exhibition illustrating the story of Tower Bridge, and the ancient steam-driven bridge control gear. Then go up the bridge (in a lift!) by the N Tower for the glass-enclosed high-level walkway. This provides some of the best river views – upstream to St Paul's and the city skyscrapers and downstream towards Greenwich. (Ideal for photographers).

As you leave the bridge on the N bank of the river go down the steps in the pavement and at the bottom turn right towards the Tower Hotel. Here follow the river front and turn left at the locks into **St Katharine's Dock**. This was once the site of a convent: the docks were built in 1828, and the modern development dates from the 1960s. The docks themselves are now used as a yacht marina. The central warehouses have been converted into luxury flats, with a shopping arcade. At the end of the lock cross to the E bank and continue around the dock. Note the large warehouse to the right. This is now *The Dickens Inn*, a great spot for a pint and a bite amidst the traditional wooden beams, barrels and sawdust. Behind the pub is the **Historic Ships Collection** (p. 64). There are seven old ships here, all open to the public, including Robert F Scott and Sir Ernest Shackleton's ship *RSS Discovery*, and the *Kathleen and May*, the last surviving topsail schooner.

From the ships go back to the pub and continue across the bridge, then turn left by the Italianate arcade of Ivory House and take the alley right through the buildings. Continue straight on until you reach the double row of free-standing Tuscan columns. Turn left there and walk straight along the dock with the *World Trade Centre*, a new business conference centre, to your right. At the end turn right and go through the small water garden and subway to **Tower Hill**, where, from 1455 until 1747, prisoners from the Tower of London were executed. Walk along the gardens until you come to the subway on the right. It leads up steps to an extant section of *Roman Wall*, built in the 2nd c. AD as part of Londinium's City Wall. From here looking E you can see the classical façade of the *Royal Mint*, where from 1811 until 1968 all the coins of the realm were minted. Retrace your steps through the subway and continue around the huge dry moat until you come to the entrance of the **Tower of London** (p. 29), the capital's most celebrated fortress, which houses the Crown Jewels.

On leaving the Tower of London turn right up Tower Hill. To the N is Tower Hill Tube Station.

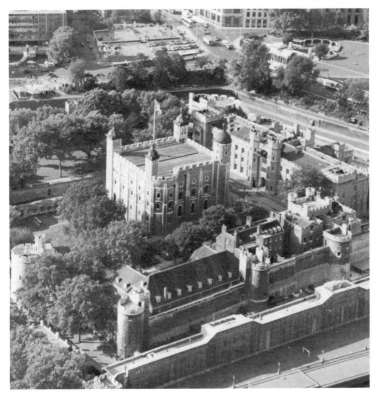

Tower of London

The Tower of London Walking Tour

For opening times, see p. 57

To subdue the population after his victory at Hastings (1066) William I built a series of strongholds throughout his new kingdom. London's fortress was the White Tower, sited at the SE corner of the city, guarding the approach from the sea. The building was later improved by Henry III, who also extended the Tower precincts, enclosing 18 acres to create an inner ward with thirteen towers around the circuit. Additionally, he created a bestiary or zoo: 3 leopards were sent by

the Holy Roman Emperor as a token of the royal arms; the King of Norway provided a white bear, and the French king an elephant. The royal zoo remained in the Lion Gate until 1831, when it was moved to Regent's Park.

Henry's son, Edward I, extended the outer defences, completely surrounding the Tower with a moat so that it could be approached by land only through the Lion Gate and by river through a watergate dedicated to Thomas à Becket. In the centuries that followed the latter was the normal entrance for state prisoners and thus acquired the name of Traitors' Gate.

Although the Norman kings had used the Tower as a power base, it was

29

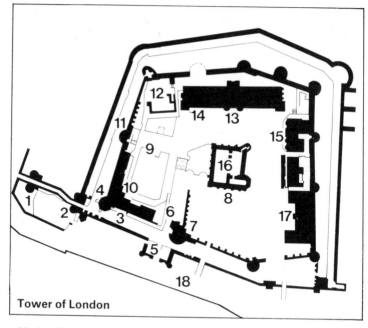

Tower of London

with the Wars of the Roses that the Tower's history became bloody and terrible. Shakespeare gave Richard Duke of Gloucester – later Richard III – the sinister appearance of a hunchback and attributed to him the murder of the saintly Henry VI, while he was at prayer in the Wakefield Tower, and of the little princes, Richard's nephews Edward V and Richard of York, in their sleep in the Bloody Tower. Henry VI's death in 1471 is commemorated annually on May 21 with sprays of white Eton lilies and red roses, laid on the traditional spot where the king, founder of Eton College and last of the Lancastrians, was murdered. But the union of the Roses under the Tudors did not halt the terror: Sir Thomas More and Bishop Fisher of Rochester were imprisoned in the Bell Tower before their execution for questioning Henry VIII's divorce from Catherine of Aragon; two of Henry's wives, Anne Boleyn and Catherine Howard, were executed on Tower Green; and Henry's daughter Elizabeth was imprisoned in the Queen's House. (She, more happily, survived to become Elizabeth I.)

But the Tower was not only a palace, a prison and a zoo, it was also the home of the royal mint until 1810 and of the royal treasure. The Crown Jewels, used at coronations and state occasions, are to be seen in the Jewel House. The Tower and its contents are guarded by Yeoman Warders, founded in 1483 by Henry VII. The 'Beefeaters' can be seen daily wearing their blue undress uniform, but on state occasions they appear splendidly attired in scarlet and gold. Every night official routine ends with the Ceremony of the Keys as the Chief Warder and escort of Foot Guards lock up the gates and towers of the medieval fortress, with the cry of 'God Preserve Queen Elizabeth'.

One of the Tower's most familiar sights is the colony of ravens which have now become one of its legends. It is said that when the ravens depart, both the White Tower and the British Commonwealth will fall.

Tour

Entrance is through the *Middle Tower* (**1**) built by Edward I and reconstructed in the 18th c., with the royal coat of arms of George I over the arch. The moat, dug by Richard I and drained in 1843, is crossed through the *Byward Tower* (**2**), 13th-c. with an 18th-19th-c. upper storey, and the **Outer Ward** (**3**) is entered.

Immediately on the left is one of the oldest towers, the *Bell Tower* (**4**) late 12th-early 13th c., topped by its belfry. Two of the many celebrated prisoners held in this tower were Sir Thomas More (1534-5) and Princess (later Queen) Elizabeth (1554). To the E, on the right, is *St Thomas's Tower* (**5**) of 1242 with beneath it the *Traitors' Gate*, through which prisoners tried at Westminster would be brought. On the left is the arched entrance of the Bloody Tower (**6**) with the round Wakefield Tower (**7**) on the right (both built by Henry III). *The Bloody Tower*, which retains its original portcullis, is believed to be the scene of the murder of the two young princes, Edward V and Richard Duke of York in 1483. Another famous prisoner of the Tower was Sir Walter Raleigh, executed in 1618. In the *Wakefield Tower* a tablet marks the traditional scene of the murder of Henry VI (1471).

The **Inner Ward** (**8**) is dominated by the White Tower, the great keep of William the Conqueror. At the top of the steps is *Tower Green* (**9**), site of the execution of many famous figures including Anne Boleyn (1536), Catherine Howard (1542), Lady Jane Grey (1554) and the Earl of Essex (1601). To the S of the green is the half-timbered 16th c. *Queen's House* (**10**) occupied by Anne Boleyn before her execution, which is now home of the Governor of the Tower. Next to it is the *Yeoman Gaoler's House*, from which Lady Jane Grey watched the

scaffold for her own execution being erected. To the W is the late 13th c. *Beauchamp Tower* (**11**), which contains graffiti and carvings made by prisoners. To the N of Tower Green is the *Chapel of St Peter ad Vincula* (**12**), founded by Henry I in the 12th c. (rebuilt in the 16th c.), burial place of Henry's beheaded queens, Anne Boleyn and Catherine Howard, and others executed on Tower Green.

Passing along the modern *Waterloo Barracks* (**13**) a door on the left admits to the Oriental Gallery containing a collection of Eastern weapons and armour (the prize exhibit is a complete suit of elephant's armour from India). From the rear of the barracks the route returns W beneath the N wall of the fortress to the *Jewel House* (**14**, adm fee) which contains the fabulous **Crown Jewels Collection**. Amongst the treasures here is Britain's oldest crown, St Edward's Crown, made for the coronation of Charles II (1661). Weighing 5lbs, the crown is still used for coronations. (For other state occasions the lighter Imperial State Crown of 1838 is used).

Before visiting the White Tower a visit may be made to the *Royal Fusiliers' Regimental Museum* (**15**) to the E. The **White Tower** (**16**), entered from the S, is the centrepiece of the great fortress. The original keep of William the Conqueror was built of grey stone, specially imported from Caen, but gained its modern name when Henry III whitewashed it in the 13th c. Henry also renovated the interior. On three floors is displayed the National Collection of Arms and Armour. On the second floor is the *Chapel Royal of St John*, with its Norman interior. Built in 1085, this is the oldest church in London.

To the E of the White Tower is a remnant of the Roman city wall. The tour continues S past the *Armouries* (**17**), through the inner wall and back to the Outer Ward. The *Tower Wharf* (**18**) to the S is the site of the artillery salute fired on the Queen's Birthday and other royal occasions.

Mayfair Walk

This walk takes you through the fashionable heart of London, past world-famous shops, buildings of historic interest and down streets which for centuries have been the haunt of the nobility and celebrities of all kinds

Starting point: Piccadilly Circus Tube Station

From the tube, take the Piccadilly (S side) exit. Here in **Piccadilly Circus** you are at the traditional heart of London. This spot is at its most spectacular during the hours of darkness, when all the neon signs are illuminated. In the centre of the Circus itself is the winged statue known as *Eros* (after the Greek God of Love, though when it was erected in 1839 it was intended to represent a rather different figure: the Angel of Christian Charity). Proceed W along the S side of **Piccadilly**, one of London's most fashionable streets. A short distance on the left is **St James's Church** (p. 42), which was designed by Sir Christopher

Wren in the 17th c. The poet William Blake was baptised here, and the basement of the Church Hall now houses London's main *Brass Rubbing Centre*. Further on is the elegant black façade of *Hatchards*, the bookshop, with its royal coats of arms above the door. This bookshop has supplied reading matter to dozens of royalty and famous personages. Lord Byron and the Duke of Wellington both had accounts here, as does the present Queen.

On the corner of Duke Street, further along, is the pale blue exterior of *Fortnum and Mason*. This is the capital's most luxurious 'store', best known for its counters of exotic delicacies such as quail's eggs and peaches in brandy. Turn left down Duke Street and you'll find the entrance to Fortnum and Mason's Soda Fountain on the corner of Jermyn Street. An ideal spot for a quick snack – but don't expect it to be cheap!

Directly across Duke Street is *Dunhill's*, the celebrated tobacconists. Pop in through the Duke Street entrance and up the narrow winding stairs to the first floor. Here you'll find the Dunhill's *Pipe Museum*, which contains over 500 pipes of all shapes and sizes and other items of smoker's bric-à-brac.

From Duke Street return to Piccadilly and cross to the imposing Renaissance-style façade of *Burlington House*. This is now the home of the **Royal Academy of Arts** (p. 68) renowned for its Summer Exhibition and other splendid exhibitions. Inside the grand entrance is a large courtyard with a statue of *Sir Joshua Reynolds*, the RA's first President.

Continue down the right-hand side of Piccadilly. Immediately after Burlington House you come to the **Burlington Arcade**. This covered walkway with its rows of elegant shops was Britain's first shopping precinct. It was privately built in 1819 and its proprietors still insist upon the rules of decorum appropriate to those far-off Regency days. A beadle in a top hat and cloak is employed to enforce the ancient by-laws which forbid whistling, singing or even hurrying! So proceed at a leisurely pace past the antique shops, jewellers and smart clothes shops until you emerge into

Burlington Gardens. Here on the right-hand side of the road is the **Museum of Mankind** (p. 66), the ethnographic branch of the British Museum which has fascinating exhibitions from all seven continents of the world. Now turn left and you come to **Bond Street**. This is Mayfair's 'High Street' and it's worth spending a little time window-gazing here. If you want to see it all, turn left and when you get to the end of the street cross the road and start back up the other side – past *Ciro's*, *Agnew's*, *The Royal Arcade* and on past such typical Mayfair stores as *Gucci's*, *Cartier's*, *Chanel* and *Aspreys*, until you come to Bruton Street on the left. Here turn left and you come to *The Coach and Horses* pub with its black and white half-timbered frontage and latticed windows. Just the place to stop off for a refreshing pint of Young's Ale. Continue down Bruton Street and you emerge into the NE side of **Berkeley Square**. This square was laid out in the early decades of the 18th c., and the plane trees in the gardens are nearly 200 years old. Entering by the gate almost opposite, cross the gardens. On the other side, the facing buildings have two blue plaques. These commemorate the fact that Clive of India and the 19th-c. statesman and Prime Minister, George Canning, lived in the square.

Turning left after the gardens, cross the street and turn left at the SW corner of the square to enter **Charles Street**. This is one of Mayfair's finest streets – particularly noted for the quiet elegance of its Georgian houses. Note the door marked 'Charles of the Ritz' and the Hungarian Embassy, both on your left, and the red-brick frontage of *The Running Footman* pub on your right. A short distance down Charles Street take the first left, heading diagonally down Queen Street. At the end cross Curzon Street and proceed through the covered alleyway into the narrow lanes and courtyards of **Shepherd Market**. In the 17th c. this was the site of the original May Fair, which gave the area its name. This fair was eventually stopped by the authorities because of 'disorderly and licentious behaviour', and to this day Shepherd Market still retains its slightly raffish character.

On entering Shepherd Market turn right and continue as far as the crossing with Hertford Street. Here you turn right, and quickly re-emerge into Curzon Street. Don't miss the cream façade of *Crewe House* across the street to the right. This restored Georgian mansion, complete with well-kept lawn and pillared front, was built in 1735 and later became the town home of the Marquess of Crewe. Proceed left down Curzon Street. At the far end of the street you can see the flags flying atop London's *Playboy Club* – where recently an Arab prince gambled away £1m in just three nights. Before you reach the Playboy Club turn right into **South Audley Street**, first noting *No 19 Curzon Street*, once the home of Benjamin Disraeli, Queen Victoria's favourite Prime Minister. The walk up South Audley Street offers glimpses, to the left, of the greenery of Hyde Park, while ahead, just over a mile away, are the distant trees of Regent's Park. From here until the end of the walk you are on the Grosvenor Estate; all the buildings and land belong to one man – the 6th Duke of Westminster – whose properties here make him the wealthiest man in the country.

Half-way along the street on the right is the **Grosvenor Chapel** with its 'colonial' architecture and fine spire. This was built in 1731, and a plaque on the front wall informs passers-by that the Armed Forces of the United States of America held their divine services here during the 1939-45 War. Behind the church is the pleasant St George's Gardens. South Audley Street is lined with quiet elegant shops – don't miss *Purdy and Sons*, the celebrated 'Gunmakers and Riflemakers', on the left at the corner of Mount Street; and should you feel like a cup of coffee try *Richoux*, further down on the right. If your diet forbids even the contemplation of their arrays of calorie-rich

creamy confectionery, you can always try their excellent scones and strawberry jam (with just a little cream).

Just beyond here South Audley Street emerges into **Grosvenor Square**. The large modern building on the left, filling the W side of the square, is the *United States Embassy*. This was designed by the Finnish-American architect Eero Saarinen and built in 1960. The golden eagle which tops the building has a wingspan of 35ft. Grosvenor Square has long been associated with the United States. In 1785 John Adams (who was later to become President) took up residence here as the first minister to Britain. On the N side of the gardens there is an impressive statue in memory of *Franklin D. Roosevelt*, our American presidential ally during the last war – and at No 20 (on the N side, at the corner of North Audley Street) General Dwight D. Eisenhower set up his headquarters in 1942. There is more of North America in the square: in the SE corner is the Canadian Embassy and in the late 1960s this was the site of the violent anti-American 'Peace in Vietnam' riots.

Leave Grosvenor Square by the NE corner and proceed E along Brook Street. On the right you'll see *Claridge's*, London's most exclusive hotel. Note the liveried doorman and the seven flagpoles – if a flag is flying it usually means that the president or king of that country is in residence. Onassis kept a permanent suite here. Past Claridge's, on the same side and just beyond South Molton Street, is a blue plaque to George Frederick Handel, the composer of *The Messiah*, who lived and died here. Turn left up the **South Molton Street** walkway. The poet William Blake once lived at *No 17*, but now it's a pedestrians-only zone full of chic shops selling the latest fashions in shirts, shoes and even sandwiches. At the end of South Molton Street you emerge into the bustle of Oxford Street close by Bond Street Tube Station.

Hampstead and Highgate

A short journey from central London brings you to the village of Hampstead, one of the most picturesque parts of the city. Lying on the side of a hill, with the beautiful and surprisingly wild Heath close by, the area has been popular with the famous and infamous for centuries. It now ranks high amongst the most coveted residential areas in London. The smart image belies Hampstead's past, for in the 16th c. washer-women settled here, making use of the abundant water supply in a flourishing laundry industry. Then, in the early 18th-c., the waters' medicinal qualities were recognized and the village became a fashionable spa. When the spa fell from favour, the area itself remained fashionable, becoming in particular the home of writers and painters such as John Keats and John Constable.

Hampstead Walk

Starting point: Hampstead
Tube Station

Leaving the station, turn immediately left down Hampstead High Street, full of stylish boutiques and cafes, and left again into **Flask Walk**. This narrow alley takes its name from the flasks in which the Hampstead water was sold. Today it contains second-hand bookshops, a bakery and coffee shop, and a Victorian pub, *The Flask*. Continuing down Flask Walk, lined with terraced cottages, you reach an open space at the far end – originally a village green on which fairs were held. To the left in New End Square is **Burgh House** (p. 47), a lovely building of 1702 which is now a community centre and museum. Close by is **Well Walk**, the road which led originally to the Long Room of the Spa, long since demolished, with its springs known as The Wells. The site of the springs is now marked by a fountain, and opposite, at *No 40*, a blue plaque marks the house of John Constable, who lived here for ten years up to his death in 1837, recording the moods of

the Heath in fine watercolours. Returning to Flask Walk, note the *Well Walk Pottery* at the corner of Gayton Road.

As a possible extension to this walk, a visit to the house lived in by the poet, John Keats, is well worthwhile (see *Keats House*, p. 65). From Flask Walk, continue into Willow Road, at the junction with Gayton Road. Follow the road downhill until it meets Downshire Hill, then turn right uphill. Shortly on the left is Keats Grove. Halfway down it on the right is **Wentworth Place**, the home of Keats for the last two years of his life. After the visit, continue up Keats Grove to Downshire Hill. At the top, turn right into Rosslyn Hill, an extension of Hampstead High Street.

Where Flask Walk meets the High Street, cross over and head for Heath Street via Oriel Place. Crossing again, you enter **Church Row**. This finely preserved street retains interesting features of 18th-c. architecture: note particularly the weatherboarding and iron brackets for holding torches. St John's, the **Hampstead Parish Church**, built in 1745, has a fine tower that was threatened with demolition when an extension to the chancel was proposed in the 19th c. Fortunately the plan was resisted by the locals and the chancel was extended unusually to the W, involving a reorientation of the altar to this end of the church. In the churchyard lie buried many famous people – John Constable, George and Gerald du Maurier, Hugh Gaitskell and others.

From Church Row, Holly Walk leads to the right up to St Mary's Church – one of the first Roman Catholic churches to be built in London – and an impressive 19th-c. terrace of houses, **Holly Place**. The former *Watch House*, used by the police on night patrol, is at the end of the terrace. At the top of the hill, turn right into Mount Vernon and then cross to Holly Bush Hill. Tucked away in a corner, in Holly Mount, stands the 17th-c. *Holly Bush Inn*, originally the stables of the house belonging to the

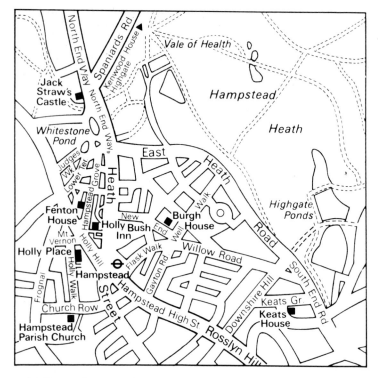

artist George Romney. Among the celebrities to have downed a pint in this inn were Oliver Goldsmith, Samuel Johnson and Charles Lamb. Romney's House was built as a studio for the artist in 1797. When Romney moved out a few years later, it became the Public Assembly Rooms in which lectures were held by Constable and Elizabeth Fry, among others. Today it has been converted into two houses, and contains no paintings by Romney. At this point it is worth making a short detour down the steps leading from Holly Mount to Heath Street. Half-way down, on the right, lies the delightful cul-de-sac, **Golden Yard**, named after the Goulding family who were tenants in the area as early as the 16th c. Some of the houses in the courtyard date from this period. The

history of the yard has been recorded on a wall plaque.

Returning to Holly Bush Hill and going up Hampstead Grove, you pass **Fenton House** (p. 48), a fine 17th-c. mansion containing a collection of historic keyboard instruments. Higher up Hampstead Grove, having passed *New Grove House*, where the writer and artist George du Maurier lived, is **Admiral's Walk**. It is named after one of George IV's admirals, Matthew Barton, who on retiring to Hampstead converted the roof of *Admiral's House* into a deck, complete with cannons. The house was immortalised by Constable in his painting *The Romantic House of Hampstead*. In the adjoining house lived John Galsworthy for 20 years: it was here that he completed *The Forsyte Saga*.

Continuing up Hampstead Grove to the top of the hill you reach **Whitestone Pond**. This is the highest point in London (437ft above sea-level). As such it offers panoramic views over the city and beyond. The pond is named after a milestone which is to be found in the bushes nearby. Constable, who lived for a short while at *No. 2 Lower Terrace*, a little way down from the pond, painted the view looking towards Hendon and Harrow from **Judges Walk**, a tree-lined avenue where, according to tradition, the assizes were held during the Great Plague. Today teams of donkeys parade here every Sunday, taking children for rides. Close by the pond is *Jack Straw's Castle*, a prominent landmark. A pub has stood on the site since 1713, but the present one was re-built in the 1960s. Jack Straw was a leader of the Peasants' Revolt of 1381. Further down North End Way lies another famous pub, the subject of a popular music hall song: *The Old Bull and Bush*. The walk ends at *Jack Straw's Castle*; but there are many other attractions in the neighbourhood.

In the valley opposite the pond is **The Vale of Health**. Once the home of washerwomen and chimney-sweeps, the Vale has also been the home of many famous writers, including D. H. Lawrence and Compton Mackenzie. Beyond the Vale, **Hampstead Heath** (p. 74) extends for 800 acres. It is pleasantly wooded and interlaced with paths. Fairs are held on the Heath on Bank Holidays, and a special children's fair by the Vale of Health on summer weekend afternoons. The Heath has three bathing ponds: one for women, one for men, the other mixed. Spaniards Road leads to *The Spaniards Inn*, built, it is said, on the site of the house of Spanish Ambassador in the reign of James I. The pub stands opposite the *Tollhouse*, which in the 17th c. marked the entrance to the Bishop of London's park which extended from Highgate to the N side of the Heath. *The Spaniards* has been associated with tales of Dick Turpin

and the Gordon rioters. Further on is **Kenwood House** (p. 65), a magnificent 18th-c. building with a superb collection of paintings and beautiful landscaped gardens, in which concerts are held in the summer. Also of interest, 200 yds E of Kenwood, is a shelter with a guide to the skyline.

Highgate

Continuing along Hampstead Lane, you reach Hampstead's neighbouring village, Highgate, famous for its **Cemetery** in which Karl Marx is buried. Viewed from afar, Highgate is reminiscent of a country village, standing as it does on the top of a hill with its church spire dominating the scene. Like Hampstead, it has had its share of famous residents, from Samuel Taylor Coleridge to Nell Gwyn. The **High Street** contains many handsome examples of 18th and 19th-c. architecture, while on Highgate Hill lies *Whittington's Stone*. Here, according to legend, Dick Whittington heard the bells of Cheapside ring out, beseeching him to return to the city. Highgate is now highly residential and contains an attractive green, **The Grove**, on which fairs used to be held. Some of the houses surrounding it date from the 16th c. The poet, Coleridge, lived in *No 3* for 19 years. The Grove still retains the character of a village green, with its 17th-c. inn, *The Flask*, frequented by Hogarth and reputedly Dick Turpin, and the **Church of St. Michael**, built in the early 19th c.

Also of interest in Highgate is **Lauderdale House**, set in Waterlow Park. The house was originally built in the 17th c. and belonged to the second Duke of Lauderdale. Charles II is said to have used it for lodging Nell Gwyn during the Duke's absence. It has been greatly altered since then and now bears more similarity to an 18th-c. country villa. It is used for exhibitions, concerts and craft demonstrations. **Waterlow Park** is a hilly park with two ponds, an aviary and secluded gardens in which plays and ballets are performed in the summer.

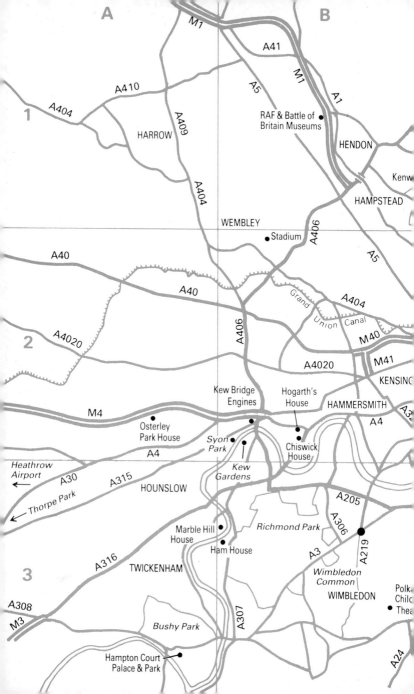

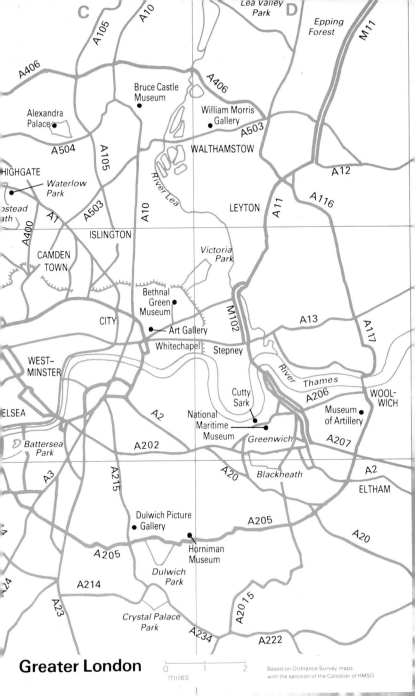

Greater London

The Best of London

Travel & Information

Tourist Information Centres

These are located in the following areas:

Victoria Station nr Platform 15
Daily 9-8.30, extended hours Jul-Aug.
Oct-May, Sun 9-5

Selfridges Oxford Street W1
Ground Floor. Open during store hours

Harrods Knightsbridge SW1
Fourth Floor. Open during store hours

British Tourist Authority
64 St James's Street SW1. Tel 499 9325
Mon-Fri 9.15-5.30, Sat 9.15-12.30.
Extended hours Apr-Sep

City Information Centre
St Paul's Churchyard EC4. Tel 606 3030
Mon-Fri 9.30-5, Sat 10-4 (Apr-Sep) &
10-12.30 (Oct-Mar)
Run by the Corporation of London:
information on the historic 'square mile'.

Telephone Information Service

Tel 730 0791. Mon-Fri 9-5 or call *What's On*
for recorded information about a selection of
events and attractions taking place in London
on 246 8041

Travel around London

Tube and Bus Information on London
Transport's tube and bus services is available
from their offices at the following tube
stations: King's Cross, Oxford Circus,
Piccadilly Circus, St James's Park, Victoria.
Telephone enquiries to 222 1234

Maps showing tube and bus services are
available free at most stations, ('Welcome to
London' maps are good for central London)

Season Tickets available from booking
offices:

Central London Rover Valid for unlimited
travel for one day on bus and tube within
central London.

Go-As-You-Please Valid for 3, 4 or 7 days for
unlimited travel on bus and tube anywhere in
London.

Red Rover (buses only) Valid for unlimited
travel for one day anywhere in London.

Green Line Buses These operate further out of
London than the red London Transport
buses. Main departure points at Marble
Arch, Hyde Park Corner, Oxford Circus and
Victoria (Information Tel 222 1234)

London's principal attractions,
described with opening times,
bus and tube services. Asterisks
indicate buildings, etc. of
outstanding interest. Map
references relate to street plan
inside cover, those marked 'GL'
to Greater London map (p. 38)

Taxis The black London taxi can be hailed in
the street when their yellow 'For Hire' sign is
lit up. They can also be hired from ranks at
major stations or booked by phone (see
Yellow Pages). Fares are metered, and a 15%
tip is usual. Mini-cab services also operate
(see Yellow Pages).

Sightseeing Tours London Transport's
Round London Sightseeing Tours offer a
circular tour (20m, 2hrs) passing most of
London's famous landmarks. Tours every
day at hourly intervals (summer 10am-7pm,
winter 10am-4pm) from Victoria (Grosvenor
Gardens), Piccadilly Circus and Marble
Arch. Booking not required.

Guided Coach Tours These are guided tours to
some of the most famous sights in London
and Southern England. Book at any Travel
Information Centre or the Wilton Road
Coach Station, Victoria SW1.

Private Guides For details of these guides and
private taxi tours contact the London Tourist
Information Centre. Tel 730 0791.

Walking Tours There are many organised
walking tours of the sights of London, many
of them devoted to specific themes.
Announcements of these walks can be found
in the daily press, the magazine *What's On &
Where To Go*, or at tourist information
centres. Some tours currently available:

Discovering London 11 Pennyfield, Warley,
Brentwood, Essex. Tel Brentwood 213704.
Walks include Jack the Ripper, the Great
Fire, Ghosts and Historic Buildings.

London Walks 139 Conway Road, Southgate
N14. Tel 882 2763. Meet at various tube
stations for 1½-2hr walks including Dickens'
London, Shakespeare's London, Pubs,
Ghosts of the West End.

The Londoner 3 Springfield Avenue N10. Tel
883 2656. Pub tours visiting four or five pubs,
leaving from Temple Tube Station at 7.30pm
on Fri.

Theatreland Tours 10 St Martin's Court, St
Martin's Lane WC2. Tel 836 8591. Two tours
– Covent Garden or South Bank – both
starting from the above address.

Churches

All Hallows by the Tower   M4
Byward Street EC3
Tube: Tower Hill. Bus: 9, 42, 78

Blitzed in 1941, now rebuilt with a copper
spire, added in 1959 to the old brick tower.
The church was largely 13th-15th-c., but
originally a Saxon foundation. A 7th-c. arch
survives at the foot of the tower. This, the
only church tower in London from the
Cromwellian period, was climbed by Samuel
Pepys during the Great Fire to witness 'the
saddest sight of desolation I ever saw'.

The rebuilt interior, the work of Lord
Mottistone, includes historic details: the
sword-rests and pulpit from the demolished
Wren church of St Swithin, a finely-carved
font cover attributed to Grinling Gibbons,
and 14th-17th-c. brasses. In this church
William Penn was baptised (1644) and John
Quincy Adams married (1797). The church
is well-known as the headquarters of the Toc
H fellowship, founded by former vicar Rev
P. B. 'Tubby' Clayton during World War I.
Records, and Roman and Saxon exhibition
in the *Crypt Museum* (see *Roman London*,
p. 60).

All Hallows on the Wall   M3
London Wall EC2
Tube: Liverpool Street. Bus: 9, 11, 279A, 502

Small church with 13th-c. foundations,
rebuilt 1765 (George Dance the Younger).
Restored after the war, it is now a Christian
Art Centre. A section of the Roman wall lies
to the W.

All Souls' Langham Place   G3
Upper Regent Street W1
Tube: Oxford Circus. Bus: 1, 3, 6, 7, 8, 12, 13, 15,
25, 53, 73, 88, 113, 137, 159, 500, 616

Neo-classical church with needle spire and
circular portico, built by John Nash, the
architect of Regent Street (1822). Intended
as a vertical visual 'stop' at the top end of the
street, the effect is now spoiled by the
buildings of Broadcasting House in the
background.

Brompton Oratory   E6
Brompton Road SW7
Tube: South Kensington. Bus: 14, 30, 74

One of London's main Roman Catholic
places of worship, this domed, Italian
Baroque-style church was completed in
1896. It was founded as the Oratory of St
Philip Neri of Rome, whose congregation
was introduced to the country by Cardinal
Newman (1847). The church has the widest
nave in England after Westminster
Cathedral and York Minster, with giant
marble statues of the Apostles on either side,
brought from Siena Cathedral (17th c.). The
church is famed for its organ music and
choral recitals.

Chapel Royal of St John   N4
White Tower, Tower of London EC3
Tube: Tower Hill. Bus: 9, 42, 78

Oldest church in London, dating from
c. 1085 (see *Tower of London* p. 31).

Chelsea Old Church, All Saints   E8
Cheyne Walk, Chelsea Embankment SW3
Tube: South Kensington then bus 45, 49. Bus: 11,
19, 22, 39

Founded in the 12th c., Chelsea's most
celebrated church was rebuilt after
near-destruction in the war. Surviving S
Chapel (1528) the work of Sir Thomas More,
whose monument is in the S wall of the
restored chancel (its fine Renaissance arch is
another survival). The church is rich in
monuments, memorials and brasses. 400
kneelers embroidered in the 1960s
commemorate great names connected with
church: Elizabeth I, Sir Thomas More, Sir
Hans Sloane and others.

Christ Church Spitalfields   N3
Commercial Street E1
Tube: Aldgate East, Liverpool Street. Bus: 67

The spire of this fine Hawksmoor church
(1723-9) dominates the area. Built at the
time when the Spitalfields silk industry
thrived following the influx of refugee
Huguenot workers. Now used for concerts.

St Bartholomew-the-Great   L3
West Smithfield EC1
Tube: Barbican, St Paul's. Bus: 4, 8, 22, 25, 141,
277, 279, 279A, 501, 502

This restored church appears externally to
be 19th-c.; it is, in fact, the oldest church in
London after St John's Chapel in the Tower.
It was founded in 1123 as a priory church by
Rahere, a courtier of Henry I who was a
canon of the Augustinian Order. Rahere also
founded London's first hospital, St
Bartholomew's, nearby. Much of the church
was destroyed during the Reformation then
remodelled in its present form.

The entrance gateway, with an
Elizabethan house above, was once the W
door of the original church: the churchyard
occupies the site of the original nave. The
present church consists of the original choir,
crossing and transepts, and one bay of the
nave. The fine Norman Romanesque can be
admired in the round arches and massive
piers. The apse and Lady Chapel are 19th-c.
reconstructions. The church has many
monuments, including one to Rahere (N of
altar). The S transept has a 15th-c. font, at
which William Hogarth was baptised.

In the precincts of the hospital, which
forms its parish, is the church of *St
Bartholomew-the-Less*, a medieval foundation
rebuilt in its unusual octagonal form in 1789
by George Dance the Younger, and again in
1823 by Thomas Hardwick. The 15th-c.
tower was preserved.

St Benet's L4
Upper Thames Street EC4
Tube: Blackfriars, Mansion House. Bus: as
St Paul's

This attractive Wren church, isolated by
feeder roads to the Blackfriars underpass,
was built 1677-85. With its dark red brick,
quoining and small cupola and steeple, it has
a Dutch appearance. The inside is well
preserved, with finely carved woodwork.
Also known as the 'Welsh Church', St
Benet's is used by Welsh Episcopalians.

St Bride's K4
Fleet Street EC4
Tube: Blackfriars. Bus: 4, 6, 9, 11, 15, 502, 513

The parish church of Fleet Street, restored
in 1957 to Wren's 17th-c. design. Only the
steeple, at 226 ft the tallest in the City,
survived wartime bombing. St Bride's
tradition of service to printers and journalists
began when Wynkyn de Worde started his
printing press 'in Fleetstrete at the signe of
the Swane' in 1500. The church, however,
goes back much further. Seven earlier
churches stood on this site: the first, Saxon,
on the foundations of an unknown Roman
building. The plan of these churches has
been determined by excavations, and the
story of the site is told in the excellent *Crypt
Museum* (Open Mon-Fri 10-4). The modern
interior is a superb replica of the Wren
original.

St Clement Danes J4
Strand WC2
Tube: Temple. Bus: 1, 4, 6, 9, 11, 13, 15, 55, 68,
77, 77A, 77C, 109, 155, 168, 170, 171, 172, 176,
184, 188, 239, 502, 513

This fine Wren church, an island in the
Strand, reminds us of the nursery rhyme
'Oranges and lemons, say the bells of St
Clement's'. Though the bells were blitzed,
they were recast and ring out the rhyme at 9
and 12 am and at 3 and 6 pm on weekdays.
The church, first built for the Danes in the
9th c., was rebuilt by Wren in 1681. After
serious war damage it was rebuilt again
(1958) as the RAF Church. Inside are many
Air Force relics, including 735 crests of units
carved in slate in the floor of the nave. Air
Forces of the Commonwealth, United States
and Polish Squadrons also commemorated.
Dr Johnson worshipped here: a statue of him
looks towards Fleet Street.

St Dunstan-in-the-West K4
Fleet Street EC4
Tube and bus: as St Clement Danes

Octagonal church of 11th-c. foundation,
rebuilt 1829-33 by John Shaw and restored
in 1950. The fine tower has an open-work
lantern: the clock of 1671 has jacks which
strike every ¼hr. Outside, over the E porch,
is a statue of Elizabeth I, made in her
lifetime.

St Ethelburga the Virgin M3
Bishopsgate EC2
Tube: Liverpool Street. Bus: 5, 6, 8, 8A, 22, 22A,
35, 47, 48, 78, 149, 243A

This tiny church has also the smallest parish
in London (3 acres). The name suggests a
Saxon foundation (Ethelburga was a 7th-c.
abbess) but the present church is 15th-c.
(arcade and W gable) to 18th-c. (belfry).
Henry Hudson the explorer, who took
communion here before he set out for the
New World in 1607, is commemorated by
three windows in the nave.

St Etheldreda's K3
Ely Place, Charterhouse Street EC1
Tube: Chancery Lane, Farringdon. Bus: 8, 18, 22,
25, 45, 46, 63, 168A, 221, 243, 259, 501

Restored in 1935, but originally the 13th-c.
chapel of Bishops of Ely, whose town house
was in Ely Place. This was the first
pre-Reformation church to be returned to
Roman Catholic authority (1874). Fine E
and W windows. The crypt, with 8ft-thick
walls, pre-dates the church.

St George's Hanover Square G4
St George's Street W1
Tube: Oxford Circus. Bus: 3, 6, 12, 13, 15, 23, 53,
88, 159, 500

Built by Wren's pupil, John James (1713-24,
restored 1894), this church is famous for
fashionable weddings. Percy Bysshe Shelley,
Benjamin Disraeli, George Eliot and
Theodore Roosevelt all married here. E
windows with early 16th c. Flemish glass
and *Last Supper* altarpiece by William Kent.
On the pavement outside are two cast-iron
game dogs by Sir Edwin Landseer RA.

St Giles Cripplegate L3
Barbican EC4
Tube: Barbican, St Paul's. Bus: 4, 147, 279A, 502

All but the 15th-17th-c. tower of this church
suffered damage on the first night of
London's Blitz. Now restored and well
integrated with the Barbican development.
Oliver Cromwell married here; John Milton
and others are buried here. Part of the
Roman city wall stands in the churchyard.

St Helen's Church M4
Great St Helen's, Bishopsgate EC3
Tube and bus: as St Ethelburga

Called 'The Westminster Abbey of the City'
because of the large number of tombs of City
dignitaries. Founded in the 13th c. as part of
St Helen's Benedictine Priory, the church is
most unusual in having two naves, separated
by an arcade (the N nave for nuns, the S for
parishioners). As well as its own memorials,
it houses many others from the nearby
church of St Martin Outwich, demolished in
1874. The church has much 17th-c. work,
including two fine doorcases and an unusual
relic – a wooden sword-rest of 1665.

Henry VII Chapel, Westminster Abbey

St James's Piccadilly G5
Piccadilly W1
Tube: Piccadilly. Bus: 3, 6, 9, 12, 13, 14, 15, 19, 22, 38, 53, 88, 159
Restored Wren church, badly damaged in the war, now popular for lunchtime sermons and organ recitals. The organ originally built for Whitehall Palace by Renatus Harris, was presented by Queen Mary in 1691. Its case was carved by Grinling Gibbons, who also carved the reredos and font.

St John's Clerkenwell K2
St John's Square EC1
Tube: Farringdon. Bus: 5, 55, 243, 277, 279
This 18th-c. building, restored after war damage, stands on the site of the 12th-c. church of the Priory of St John, in the square which was once the priory courtyard. (The priory itself, which belonged to the Knights of St John of Jerusalem, now survives only in its gatehouse – St John's Gate – in St John's Lane S of Clerkenwell Road). The crypt of the church, the only surviving part of the Norman building, is still used by the Order of St John and the Ambulance Brigade.

St John the Evangelist H6
Smith Square SW1
Tube: Westminster. Bus: 3, 10, 77, 77A, 88, 149, 159, 168, 507
Baroque church, built by Thomas Archer in 1714-28, gutted by bombing and now restored as a concert hall and exhibition centre. Its four towers are said to have been suggested by Queen Anne, who showed Archer an upturned footstool.

St Lawrence Jewry L4
King Street EC2 (next to Guildhall)
Tube: Bank, Moorgate. Bus: 6, 8, 9, 11, 15, 21, 22, 23, 25, 43, 76, 133, 501, 502, 513
Official church of the City Corporation, in the shadow of Guildhall. A Wren building (1670-87) faithfully rebuilt after bomb damage.

St Magnus the Martyr M4
Lower Thames Street EC3
Tube: Monument. Bus: 8A, 10, 27, 35, 40, 43, 44, 47, 48, 95, 133, 501, 513
Wren church (1671-8) with fine tower topped by a cupola and small spire, worth seeking out. Its Baroque interior, restored in 1951 after war damage, has some fine fittings, including two 17th-c. doorcases converted into altars at the head of each aisle, and beautifully carved altarpiece, organ loft and pulpit.

St Margaret's Westminster H6
Parliament Square SW1
Tube and bus as Westminster Abbey
The House of Commons' parish church is also a fashionable venue for weddings. Among those married here were Samuel

Pepys (1655) and Winston Churchill (1908).
The church was founded c. 12th c. and
rebuilt in the 16th c. The present facing of
Portland stone is 18th-c. The magnificent
15th-c. Flemish glass in the E window was
the gift of Ferdinand and Isabella of Spain to
Henry VII on the bethrothal of Prince
Arthur to their daughter, Catherine of
Aragon. The stained glass windows in the S
aisle are by John Piper. There are many
monuments and memorials including one to
William Caxton (d. 1491, also buried here)
and another to the Parliamentarians John
Pym, Robert Blake and others whose bodies
were thrown into a pit here by the Royalists.

St Martin-in-the-Fields H4
Trafalgar Square WC2
Tube: Charing Cross. Bus: 1, 3, 6, 9, 11, 12, 13,
15, 23, 24, 29, 53, 77, 77A, 88, 159, 170, 172, 176
This landmark near the National Gallery,
with its fine Corinthian portico and spire, is
part of London life. Memorial services for
the acting profession are usually held here,
and unemployed and down-and-outs are
always welcomed. Lunchtime concerts are a
great attraction, and the steps leading to the
portico are a popular meeting place.
    The first church was built here in the 13th
c: the present building, the work of Wren's
pupil James Gibbs, was completed in 1726.
St Martin's is the parish church of the
Admiralty and the Sovereign, whose London
home – Buckingham Palace – is in its
bounds. The Royal Arms of George I – St
Martin's first churchwarden – are above the
portico, and the weathervane on the spire is
topped by a crown.

St Mary Aldermary L4
Queen Victoria Street EC4
Tube: Mansion House. Bus: 6, 8, 9, 11, 15, 21, 22,
23, 25, 43, 76, 133, 501, 513
Like 17 other churches in the City's square
mile, St Mary Aldermary was destroyed first
in the Great Fire and then by the Blitz.
When Sir Christopher Wren rebuilt the
church in 1682, he used as much of the old
stone as possible to construct a copy of the
1511 church. The original building was
Gothic, seen in the tower (the lower part
survived the Great Fire) and the handsome
interior with its plaster fan vaulting. The
pulpit, doorcases and font survive from the
17th c.

St Mary-le-Bow L4
(Bow Church) Bow Lane, EC4
Tube: Bank, Mansion House. Bus: as St Mary
Aldermary
Wren's Bow Bells church (1670-83) restored
after bomb damage, has a beautiful tower,
the spire surmounted by a weathervane in
the form of a griffin. The bells are the
modern successors of the original Bow Bells,
destroyed in the Great Fire. These were the

legendary bells which summoned Dick
Whittington back to London, to become
Lord Mayor. Those born within the sound
of them are thought of as Cockneys, the real
Londoners. The new E windows by John
Hayward are in the modern style. The crypt
(1080-90) is the oldest ecclesiastical building
in London after the Chapel Royal, Tower of
London. Its Norman arches, or 'bows' gave
the church its name. The Appeal Court of
the Archbishop of Canterbury, the 'Court of
Arches' was originally held here.

St Mary-le-Strand J4
Strand WC2
Tube: Temple. Bus: as St Clement Danes
Like St Clement Danes, this perfect little
Baroque church is an island in the midst of
the Strand traffic. Completed in 1717 by
James Gibbs, the church has a fine steeple.

St Marylebone F3
Marylebone Road NW1
Tube: Baker Street. Bus: 1, 2, 2B, 13, 18, 18A, 27,
30, 74, 113, 159, 176
Parish church by Thomas Hardwick (1813)
with fine classical portico, facing York Gate,
Regent's Park. Robert Browning and
Elizabeth Barrett were married here in 1846.

St Michael Cornhill M4
Cornhill EC3
Tube: Bank. Bus: as St Mary Aldermary
A Wren church of 1677, restored and
'Victorianised' by Sir George Gilbert Scott
(1857-60). The handsome Gothic tower was
added in 1722 by Nicholas Hawksmoor.

St Pancras H2
Upper Woburn Place WC1
Tube: Euston, Euston Square. Bus: 14, 18, 30, 68,
73, 77, 77A, 77C, 170, 188, 239
The inspiration of ancient Greece,
heightened at the time by the archaeological
trophies brought from Athens by Lord
Elgin, shows in this classical temple by
W. and H. Inwood (1822). Most striking
features are the W portico, the octagonal
tower based on Athens' Tower of the Winds,
and caryatid porticoes at the E end based on
that of the Erectheion on the Athenian
acropolis.

St Paul's Covent Garden J4
Covent Garden WC2
Tube: Covent Garden. Bus: 1, 6, 9, 13, 15, 23, 24,
29, 77, 77A, 170, 176
On the W side of the market piazza, this
church was commissioned by the Earl of
Bedford for his estate with an order to the
architect Inigo Jones that it should be kept
simple – 'not much better than a barn'. For
Jones it was to be 'the handsomest barn in
Europe'. Completed in 1633 it was gutted by
fire in 1795 and restored by Philip
Hardwick. Main features are the preserved
grand E portico and barn-like roof. The

porticoed E end, facing the piazza, has the appearance of the front of the church: it is actually the rear and the front is approached through the garden on the W side. The church is associated with actors, many of whom have memorials here.

★ St Paul's Cathedral   L4
St Paul's Churchyard EC4

Tube: St Paul's, Mansion House. Bus: 4, 6, 8, 9, 11, 15, 18, 22, 23, 25, 76, 141, 501, 502, 513. Oct-Easter 7.30-5, Easter-Sep 7.30-7. Ambulatory, Crypt, Whispering Gallery & Dome: Mon-Fri 10-4.15, Sat 11-4.15, closed Sun (adm fees). Super Tours of Cathedral at 11 & 2, not Sun

For description and tour, see p. 22

St Stephen Walbrook   M4
Walbrook EC4

Tube: Bank, Cannon Street. Bus: as St Mary Aldermary. Closed for restoration.

The Lord Mayor's church, next to the Mansion House. This Wren building (1679) has a particularly fine interior with a dome supported by eight arches on Corinthian pillars, a model for the architect's greatest work, St Paul's Cathedral. The dome, destroyed by bombing, has been finely restored. The N wall has a painting of the Martyrdom of St Stephen by the American artist Benjamin West. The church is now the home of the Samaritans, set up to counsel the suicidal and despairing.

Savoy Chapel   J4
Savoy Street, Strand WC2 (Queen's Chapel of the Savoy)

Tube: Temple, Charing Cross. Bus: as St Clement Danes Tue-Fri 11-3.30 Sun 11-12.45

This chapel is all that survives of Savoy Palace, given by Henry III in 1246 to his wife's uncle, the Count of Savoy. Later, the palace passed to John of Gaunt, Duke of Lancaster, whose son Bolingbroke took over the Lancastrian estates and the title when he succeeded to the throne as Henry IV. The palace, burnt down in the Peasants' Revolt of 1381, was rebuilt in 1505, but the chapel is the only part to survive, restored after a fire in 1864. The late Perpendicular style of the original building was carefully retained. The royal pews remind us that this is the Sovereign's chapel, and the Queen's title of Duke of Lancaster is recognised in the special version of the National Anthem sung here: 'God save our gracious Queen, Long live our noble Duke ...'

This is also the Chapel of the Royal Victorian Order.

Southwark Cathedral   M5
Borough High Street SE1

Tube: London Bridge. Bus: 8A, 10, 18, 27, 35, 40, 43, 44, 47, 48, 70, 95, 133, 501, 513

At the S end of London Bridge, this splendid building was the first of the Gothic (Early English) style in London. It is the mother church of the diocese of Southwark, including most of S London and part of Surrey. A 7th-c. foundation, later a 12th-c. Augustinian priory church, the Norman building was burned down and replaced by the Gothic church. Surviving from this building (13th-c.) are the crossing, lower part of the tower, choir and ambulatories, and retro-choir (Lady Chapel). The transepts were added in the 14th c., the upper part of the tower was rebuilt in 1520. After the Dissolution the priory church, dedicated to St Mary Overy, became the parish church of St Saviour. The nave was rebuilt in the late 19th c. and the church was granted cathedral status in 1905. Interior details include a memorial to Shakespeare (1912) in the S aisle with a stained glass window above showing characters from his plays; Harvard Chapel (1907) in memory of the founder of Harvard University, born in the parish; and an altarpiece by Sir Ninian Comper (1929).

Temple Church   K4
Inner Temple Lane EC4

Tube: Temple. Bus: as St Clement Danes

Restored with loving care after wartime destruction, this round church of the Knights Templars now serves two Inns of Court, the Middle and Inner Temple. Its unusual circular nave of 1185 was based on the plan of the Church of the Holy Sepulchre, Jerusalem: the rib-vaulted chancel in the Early English style was added in 1240. The late Norman doorway has been well restored, as have all the interior details. Interesting are the 13th-c. effigies of the Knights on the floor of the nave and the grotesque heads on the spandrels of the arches, representing souls in heaven and in hell. The reredos (1682) is by Sir Christopher Wren.

★ Westminster Abbey   H6
Parliament Square SW1

Tube: Westminster. Bus: 3, 11, 12, 24, 29, 53, 70, 76, 77, 77A, 77C, 88, 109, 155, 159, 168, 170, 172, 184, 503. Daily 7.30-6; Choir & Royal Chapels: Mon-Fri 9.20-4, Sat 9.20-2 & 3.45-5, closed Sun, adm fee. Chapter House: Apr-Sep, 9.30-5, Oct-Mar 9.30-4, adm fee. Museum: 10.30-4, adm fee. Super Tours of the Abbey every 50 min, not Sun

For description and tour, see p. 16

Westminster Cathedral   G6
Ashley Place SW1

Tube: Victoria. Bus: 2, 2B, 10, 11, 16, 16A, 24, 25, 29, 36, 36A, 36B, 38, 39, 52, 70, 76, 149, 185, 500, 503, 507
Tower 10.30-dusk. Adm fee

England's major Roman Catholic church is the seat of the Cardinal Archbishop of Westminster. Built 1895-1903 in the Byzantine Romanesque style it has a tower, 284ft high, which is still a London landmark, despite the encroaching Victoria

Street developments. A break in the building line at the S end of Victoria Street allows a good view of the impressive brick and stone facade; the interior is also of brick. The cathedral has the widest nave in England (60ft, or 149ft with the side aisles and chapels) with a central dome of 117ft. Much of the marble used in the cathedral was taken from the quarry which supplied the great 6th c. basilica of St Sophia in Constantinople. Outstanding among many finely decorated chapels is the Lady Chapel, the first part of the cathedral to be completed. The main piers have bas-reliefs of the 14 Stations of the Cross, carved by Eric Gill.

Historic Buildings & Monuments

Apsley House
See *Wellington Museum* p. 70

Bank of England
M4
Threadneedle Street EC2
Tube: Bank. Bus: 6, 8, 9, 11, 15, 21, 22, 23, 25, 43, 76, 133, 501, 502, 513
'The Old Lady of Threadneedle Street' the world's largest bank, is a solid blank-faced building in the City of London. The oldest part of the present building is the external wall, relieved by classical columns, which was the work of Sir John Soane, appointed architect of the bank in 1788. The buildings were completed in 1833 and remodelled internally in 1924-39. Only the entrance hall – in the charge of gate-keepers in pink tails, scarlet waistcoats and toppers – is open to the public. The Bank of England, set up by royal charter in 1694, has both a national role as banker to the Government and domestic banks and an international role as banker to many overseas banks. The vaults hold the country's gold reserves.

Banqueting House
H5
Whitehall SW1
Tube: Charing Cross, Westminster. Bus: 3, 11, 12, 24, 29, 53, 77, 77A, 88, 159, 170, 172. Tue-Sat 10-5, Sun 2-5. Closed Jan 1, Good Fri, Dec 25 & 26. Adm fee
This splendid classical building is the only remaining part of the great palace of Whitehall. In 1619 the Banqueting House was destroyed by fire and James I commissioned Inigo Jones to erect a new one. The hall is based on the model of a Roman basilica and has magnificent *ceiling paintings* by Rubens (1635) representing the Apotheosis of James I and an allegory of the Birth of Charles I. Ironically, the Banqueting House was chosen for the site of Charles I's execution. Visitors can see the site of the window (on the staircase) from which the king stepped onto the scaffold on Jan 29, 1649.

St Paul's Cathedral

Buckingham Palace
G6
The Mall SW1
Tube: Green Park, St James's Park, Hyde Park Corner, Victoria. Bus: 2, 2B, 9, 10, 11, 14, 16, 16A, 19, 22, 24, 25, 29, 30, 36, 36A, 36B, 38, 39, 52, 73, 74, 76, 137, 149, 185, 500, 503, 507
The principal residence of the sovereign, dominating the Mall and backed by a garden of 40 acres. Buckingham House, property of the Duke of Buckingham, originally stood on this site; it was purchased for George III in 1762. The present building is the work of John Nash (1830) with the addition of an E wing (1846) forming a quadrangle. This E front, seen from the Mall, was restyled in 1913 by Sir Aston Webb, with the splendid façade of Portland stone we see today. The forecourt of the palace is the scene of the famous Changing of the Guard ceremony in the mornings (see *Ceremonies & Events*, p. 78).

Burgh House
See Hampstead map
New End Square, Hampstead NW3
Tube: Hampstead. Bus: 210, 268. Wed-Sat 12-5 Bank Hol Mons 2-5. Closed Jan 1, Good Fri, 1st Mon in May, Dec 25 & 26.
This elegant Queen Anne building is one of the oldest in Hampstead. Originally the home of the Rev. Burgh, a composer of church music, it is now a community centre and museum. It also has an art gallery and a study centre. The interior of the house has been little altered: for example, the Music Room, where concerts are held today, contains some beautiful original panelling in pinewood. There are constantly changing exhibitions focussed on Hampstead life, past and present.

Chelsea Royal Hospital
F8
Royal Hospital Road, Chelsea SW3
Tube: Sloane Square. Bus: 11, 39, 137. Mon-Sat 10-5.30, Sun 2-5.30. Closed Good Fri, Easter Sun, 1st Mon in May, Dec 24-26
This home for veteran and invalid soldiers – the Chelsea Pensioners – was founded in 1682 by Charles II. The original inmates were veterans of Britain's first standing army, set up during the Commonwealth. The buildings, designed by Sir Christopher Wren (with later additions by Robert Adam and Sir John Soane) are grouped round a central quadrangle in which stands a bronze statue of the king by Grinling Gibbons. About 400 pensioners live in the hospital and wear a uniform dating from the time of Marlborough – scarlet frock coats in summer and dark blue greatcoats in winter. On Oak Apple Day (May 29) the Pensioners have a special parade to celebrate the restoration of Charles II.
The buildings that are open to the public include the *Chapel* and *Museum*, and the *Great Hall*, used as a dining hall by the Pensioners. Many royal portraits adorn the panelled walls, together with flags and

commemorative panels of Pensioners who took part in battles from 1662 to the Korean War. Visitors can also explore the various courts and the attractive *Ranelagh Gardens* running down to the Chelsea Embankment.

Chiswick House
GL B2

Burlington Lane, Chiswick W4

Tube: Chiswick Park or Turnham Green then bus E3; Hammersmith then bus 290. Bus: 27, 91, 237, 267, 290, E3. Daily 9.30-1, 2-6.30 (4 pm mid-Oct to mid-Mar)

This attractive mansion in its spacious gardens was built to the design of its owner, the 3rd Earl of Burlington. Lord Burlington was an admirer of the 16th-c. Italian architect Andrea Palladio and followed his strictly classical style in the creation of this small domed villa, completed in 1729. The building was not intended as a residence but as a Temple of Arts, where Burlington could entertain his friends. There are two floors: the low-ceilinged ground floor and the lofty upper floor, reached by balustraded steps on either side of the building.

The interior, decorated by William Kent, is particularly fine and has as its centrepiece the *Domed Saloon*, an octagonal room crowned by a panelled dome. Around it are other beautifully decorated rooms and the gallery, which runs the whole length of the house. There are paintings by Guido Reni, Peter Lely and Godfrey Kneller. The gardens were laid out by Kent and contain a gateway by Inigo Jones – an earlier disciple of Palladio – brought from Beaufort House in Chelsea.

Clarence House
G5

The Mall SW1

Tube and bus as for Buckingham Palace

The London home of Queen Elizabeth the Queen Mother. Not open to the public and only visible from the Mall, this fine Georgian house was built for the Duke of Clarence, later William IV, in 1825. Despite the completion of Buckingham Palace, William subsequently lived here as monarch. Before her accession as Queen (1952), Princess Elizabeth lived here with the Duke of Edinburgh. Princess Anne was born here (1950) and the Princess of Wales stayed here (1981) after the announcement of her engagement.

Cleopatra's Needle
J4

Victoria Embankment WC2

Tube: Charing Cross, Embankment. Bus: 109, 155, 184

This pink granite obelisk, almost 69ft high, was the gift of the Egyptian Viceroy, Mohammed Ali, to Britain in 1819. It was not sent to London, however, until 1878, after a hazardous voyage in a specially constructed iron pontoon, towed by a steamer. The obelisk is one of a pair erected *c*. 1500 BC at Heliopolis by Thothmes III,

and is inscribed with a record of the deeds of Thothmes and of Rameses the Great (it has no connection with Cleopatra). The companion obelisk was erected in Central Park, New York.

Crosby Hall
D8

Cheyne Walk, Chelsea

Tube: South Kensington then bus 45, 49. Bus: 11, 19, 22, 39. Daily 10-12 & 2-5. Closed Dec 25 & 26

This 1927 building, the hostel of the Federation of British University Women, incorporates (E side) part of a 15th-c. merchant's house. This building, erected by Sir John Crosby, originally stood in Bishopsgate. In the 17th c. the building burned down, with the exception of the great hall which survived and was moved to its present site (once Sir Thomas More's Chelsea garden) at the beginning of this century. It is now used as a dining hall and has a fine oak roof, musicians' gallery and oriel window. The house passed from Crosby to Richard, Duke of Gloucester, who held court here while Edward V was in the Tower.

The Dutch House
See *Kew Palace* p. 52

Fenton House
See Hampstead map

Hampstead Grove, Hampstead NW3

Tube: Hampstead. Bus: 268, 270. Apr-Oct, Mon-Wed, Sat & Bank Hol Mon 11-5, Sun 2-5. Feb, Mar & Nov, Sat & Sun 2-5. Closed Dec & Jan. Adm fee

Built in 1693, and claimed to be the oldest surviving mansion in Hampstead, this gracious building with its walled, sunken garden still retains the atmosphere of a private house. As well as containing a large collection of furniture and porcelain, Fenton House is noted for its fine array of early keyboard instruments, including 17th-c. harpsichords and 18th-c. spinets.

Gray's Inn WC1
J3

Tube: Chancery Lane. Bus: 8, 18, 19, 22, 25, 38, 45, 46, 55, 171, 172, 501. *Gardens* May-Jul, Mon-Fri 12-2; Aug-Sep, Mon-Fri 9.30-5. Closed Dec 24-Jan 1, Easter & Spring Bank Hol. *Hall, Chapel & Library* Apply to Under-Treasurer

One of the four Inns of Court, founded as a law school in 1370. Entered from the N side of Holborn, through a 17th-c. gateway. The mainly 17th and 18th-c. buildings were badly damaged in the war but have been faithfully restored. On the N side of South Square is the *Elizabethan Hall* where Queen Elizabeth I was entertained with masques and Shakespeare first performed his *Comedy of Errors*. Another great Elizabethan associated with Gray's Inn was its treasurer, Sir Francis Bacon, the statesman and essayist, who lived here for 50 years. Other attractive features are *Gray's Inn Square*, with access from Gray's Inn Road, and the *Gardens*, laid out in about 1600.

Guildhall L3
King Street EC2

Tube: Bank. Bus: as Bank of England. *Great Hall*
Daily 10-5. Closed Sun Oct-Apr, Jan 1, Good Fri,
Easter weekend, Dec 25 & 26, and for functions.
Art Gallery Only open for special exhibitions.
Reference Library Mon-Sat 9.30-5. Closed Jan 1,
Good Fri, Easter Sat & Mon, 1st Mon in May,
Spring & Late Summer Hol Mon, Dec 24-26. *Clock Museum* Same times as library but closed Sat.

For a thousand years the Guildhall has been
the seat of local government for the City of
London and its ceremonial centre. The
present hall, replacing an earlier one,
belongs to the 15th c., but little remains of
the original structure. Twice in its history
the building has been gutted, by the Great
Fire of London and World War II bombs.
Since the war there have been many new
extensions.

The porch of the gatehouse, dominated by
the City's coat-of-arms, retains its 15th-c.
vaulting. The *Great Hall* is a splendid
chamber which was largely rebuilt after the
Great Fire with further restoration in the
19th c.; the roof was replaced in 1954 by Sir
Giles Gilbert Scott, who also installed the
stained glass windows with names of former
Mayors and Lord Mayors. Shields and
banners of the livery companies ornament
the hall, along with the monuments of many
famous men including Lord Nelson, the
Duke of Wellington and Sir Winston
Churchill. Beneath the hall is the 15th-c.
Crypt, restored in 1961. Other buildings
include the modern Livery Hall, also by
Scott, the old and new *Guildhall Library*
(with its Clock Museum) and the *Guildhall Art Gallery*.

Ham House GL B3
Richmond, Surrey

British Rail or Tube: Richmond then bus 65, 71.
Apr-Sep, 2-6; Oct-Mar, Tue-Sun & Bank Hols
12-4. Adm fee

Built in 1610 for Sir Thomas Vavasour, this
fine riverside mansion was much altered in
the later 17th c. by its subsequent owners,
the Duke and Duchess of Lauderdale. It
presents a striking picture of the courtly life
of the 17th-c. aristocracy, retaining much of
its original furniture and interior ornament.
Lauderdale, a member of Charles II's Cabal,
was an ambitious man and his desire for
grandeur, shared by his wife, is shown in the
imposing red-brick exterior of the building
that they enlarged.

The interior is also sumptuous, with fine
ceilings, woodwork, tapestries,
chimney-pieces and furniture. Much of the
work is by Dutch artists and craftsmen,
including marine paintings by William Van
de Velde. The principal ceilings were
executed by Antonio Verrio, who also
worked at Windsor Castle and Hampton
Court Palace. There are two portraits of the
Duchess by Sir Peter Lely.

★ Hampton Court Palace GL A3
Middlesex

British Rail: Hampton Court or boat from
Westminster Pier (summer only). Bus: 111, 131,
211, 216, 267, MV7. Green Line 715, 718, 725,
726. Apr-Sep, Mon-Sat 9.30-6, Sun 11-6; Oct-Mar
closes at 5. Closed Dec 24, 25 & Easter Bank Hol

On the N bank of the Thames about 12m SE
of central London, this is one of the capital's
most popular excursions. The palace was not
originally a royal residence but was built as a
country house in 1514 by Thomas Wolsey,
who in that year became Archbishop of York
and in the following year Cardinal and
Henry VIII's Lord Chancellor. By 1525,
however, Wolsey's power was in decline and
in an attempt to regain Henry VIII's favour
he presented Hampton Court to the king.
Henry enlarged the building, converting it
into one of his most magnificent palaces, a
fitting backcloth to the splendour of his
court. Not only did he build the Great Hall,
Chapel Royal and State Apartments, but he
also laid out fine formal gardens and for his
sport a deer park, a tilt-yard and a real tennis
court.

The palace was a favourite retreat for
Henry's children and the Stuart kings, but
when William and Mary came to the throne
in 1689 they decided to make Hampton
Court their principal home. Sir Christopher
Wren was duly commissioned to 'beautify
and add some new building to that fabric,
their majesties taking great delight in it.'
Wren pulled down the Tudor buildings of
Cloister Green Court, replacing them with a
palace of graceful classical style with cloisters
enclosing what is now Fountain Court.
Within this new building he laid out the
King's Apartments on the S side, and the
Queen's on the N and E. The old Tudor
formal gardens were swept away and
replaced by the Great Fountain Garden, the
Wilderness, the Maze, the Broad Walk and
other gardens in the Baroque fashion of the
day.

Wren planned to demolish the rest of the
Tudor palace and create a great Baroque
building but, apart from the laying out of a
grand Chestnut Avenue in Bushy Park as an
approach, this scheme was never carried out.
Instead Sir John Vanbrugh refurbished a
suite in the NE corner of the palace for
Frederick, Prince of Wales in the 1720s, and
a decade later William Kent built the
Cumberland Suite in the Clock Court for
George II's second son. But Hampton
Court's days as a great royal palace were
numbered: George III never resided here
and early in Victoria's reign the buildings
were opened to the public.

Tour
The entrance is over the moat flanked by
royal beasts and through the *Great Gatehouse*
(rebuilt by George II). This leads into the

Hampton Court Palace

Base Court, resembling an Oxford college quad, with Tudor chambers. Facing is the Tudor *Clock Gatehouse* also known as *Anne Boleyn's Gateway*, with towers embellished by terracotta medallions of Roman emperors by Giovanni Maiano, and the arms of Thomas Wolsey over the entrance. Passing through the gatehouse into the *Clock Court*, the inner front is topped by an astronomical clock built by Nicolas Oursian, who was Henry VIII's astronomer.

On the SE side of Clock Court is the entrance to Wren's **State Apartments** for King William. Ascent is made by the *King's Staircase*, adorned with ceiling paintings by Antonio Verrio (1700), via the *King's Guardroom* with its armoury collection, to the *King's Apartments*. The sequence of rooms is from the most public (The King's First Presence Chamber) to the most private (Bedroom, Dressing Room and Writing Closet). Parallel to the King's Apartments, overlooking Fountain Court, is the *Cartoon Gallery* built by Wren to house the Raphael Cartoons, one of the great art treasures of Charles I (these are tapestry copies; the originals are in the V & A). From the King's Apartments proceed through the E and N sides of the court, containing the *Queen's Gallery & Apartments* and a range of private chambers built for *George II* in 1732.

Beyond the Queen's Apartments is the **Chapel Royal** built by Wolsey and enlarged by Henry VIII, who built the King's Pew. Behind the King's Pew runs the gallery supposed to be haunted by Catherine Howard, the fifth wife of Henry. She was under house arrest for suspected adultery and tried to reach the king in his pew to beg for mercy. Unhappily she was dragged back by the soldiers and subsequently executed on Tower Green (1542).

Nearby is *Wolsey's Closet*, the only remaining room furnished in the style of the Cardinal's house. It has linenfold panelling on the lower part of the walls with panels of New Testament scenes above. The ceiling has Renaissance plasterwork with Tudor roses. The main part of Henry's Palace consists of the *Great Watching Chamber* and the **Great Hall**, where he held his masques and feasts. The magnificent hammerbeam roof is decorated with painted ornaments, including Anne Boleyn's initials and falcon device dating it to 1533-36. Also in this section of the palace are the *Great Tudor Kitchens*.

Also worth visiting is the *Orangery*, housing the paintings *The Triumph of Caesar* by Mantegna (1485-1495). Special features of the gardens, open to the public, are the Maze, Wilderness, Privy Garden and Pond Garden. Not to be missed is the *Great Vine*, planted in 1768 and still bearing fruit.

★ Houses of Parliament J6

Palace of Westminster, Westminster SW1
Tube: Westminster. Bus: 3, 11, 12, 24, 29, 53, 70, 76, 77, 77A, 77C, 88, 109, 155, 159, 168, 170, 172, 184, 503. *Admission during sessions* House of Commons: Mon-Thur 2.30-rise of House (not before 10.30 pm), Fri 9.30-3. House of Lords: Mon-Thur 2.30-10 pm

The other name for the Houses of Parliament – the Palace of Westminster – is a reminder of an historic building that once stood on this site. This was one of the royal palaces of the English monarch, from the 11th c. until Henry VIII moved his court to Whitehall Palace (1529) and St James's Palace (1536). Of the original palace only Westminster Hall and two other buildings survive: the rest were destroyed by fire in 1834.

The parliamentary tradition began when Westminster Hall was used for the meetings of the Great Council, the predecessor of Parliament and the Courts of Justice. In the 1550s, when the buildings were no longer used as a royal palace, the two houses commenced their sittings here. In 1605 an attempt was made by Guy Fawkes and other Catholic conspirators to blow up the House of Lords when James I was opening Parliament: the 'Gunpowder Plot' failed and Nov 5 – Guy Fawkes' Night – is still celebrated with firework displays. The vaults of the Houses of Parliament, where the gunpowder was planted, are still searched every year by the Yeomen of the Guard before the State Opening of Parliament.

The present building, the Gothic masterpiece of Sir Charles Barry, was commissioned, and opened in 1852. World War II bombs destroyed the House of Commons: this was rebuilt after the war and reopened in 1950.

The building contains 11 courtyards and about 1200 rooms connected by two miles of passages. At the heart of the building is the *Central Lobby*, reached from *St Stephen's Hall Entrance* on the W side. This is the way into the building for those wishing to visit either of the chambers. To the S of the Central Lobby is the *House of Lords*, the upper chamber to which legislation by the lower chamber, the Commons, is referred. The Lords, whose members are either hereditary or life peers, also has a judicial function as the highest Court of Appeal. The elaborate Gothic chamber, with the monarch's throne on a dais, was decorated by A. W. Pugin. To the N of the Central Lobby is the *House of Commons*, the lower and effectively the ruling chamber of the Houses of Parliament. Its 630 members are elected for a maximum of five years, although the life of a Parliament can be considerably less, depending on the strength of the ruling party's majority. The rebuilt chamber is the work of Sir Giles Gilbert Scott (1948-50) on the lines of the Barry original.

Dominating the S end of the building is the *Victoria Tower*, at 336 x 75ft the tallest and largest square tower in the world. Its archway serves as the royal entrance to the Lords, used by the monarch for the State Opening of Parliament. (This ceremony recalls the fact that although the Palace of Westminster has not been occupied by a monarch since the time of Henry VIII, it is still one of the Queen's palaces. Parliament sits here at the monarch's request, and every year the Queen carries out this official opening, one of her major public duties.) Other prominent features of the building are the *Central Spire* (300ft) and the Clock Tower to the N, known as *Big Ben* (320ft). Correctly, this name applies not to the clock or tower but to the great bell (weight 13½ tons) whose chimes are a familiar introduction to BBC radio news.

Between the Palace Yards, facing Parliament Square, is the historic **Westminster Hall**, the only surviving major building of the medieval Palace of Westminster. Built originally by William II (1099) it was restored in the reign of Richard II (1399), when Henry Yevele added the splendid and massive hammerbeam roof. From the 12th to the 19th c. this great hall was used as the meeting place of the Courts of Justice, and it was here that Sir Thomas More, Guy Fawkes and Charles I were all tried and sentenced to death. Today the hall is used for conferences and for the lying-in-state of monarchs. Stairs at one corner lead to *St Stephen's Crypt*, which also survived the fire of 1834. This was originally the crypt of St Stephen's Chapel (now St Stephen's Hall) which was destroyed in the fire. The chapel here, colourfully restored by Charles Barry and Augustus Pugin, is used by the members.

Inns of Court

The early law schools that existed in the 12th and 13th c. were formed into societies known as the Inns of Court. Those that survive are Gray's Inn, Lincoln's Inn, Inner Temple and Middle Temple (see entries), all located near Chancery Lane. The Inns were modelled on the colleges of Oxford and Cambridge, each with its Hall, Library, Chapel, 'quad' and chambers. Barristers and students maintain the tradition of dining together in Hall, to preserve the unity of their association. England's two most famous writers have associations with the Inns: William Shakespeare's plays were performed in the Halls of Gray's Inn and Middle Temple in his lifetime and Charles Dickens, who was briefly a clerk in Lincoln's Inn, used them as a setting for some of the scenes in his novels.

Jewel Tower H6
Old Palace Yard SW1
Tube and bus as Houses of Parliament. Mon-Sat
9.30-1 & 2-6.30 (4pm Oct-Mar), Closed Jan 1,
Good Fri, 1st Mon in May, Dec 24-26

Built in 1366 by Henry Yevele, who rebuilt
the W end of the nave of Westminster Abbey
and the roof of Westminster Hall, this
moated tower across the road from the
Houses of Parliament once formed the SW
corner of the royal Palace of Westminster.
The tower was used as the treasury for the
jewels, plate and private valuables of Edward
III (since dispersed). Exhibits include a
Saxon sword discovered in 1948 during
excavations and cases showing the standard
weights and measures (the tower was used by
the Weights and Measures Department from
1869-1938).

Kensington Palace C5
The Broad Walk,
Kensington Gardens W8
Tube: High Street Kensington, Queensway. Bus:
9, 9A, 12, 27, 28, 31, 33, 49, 52, 73, 88. Mon-Sat
9-3, Sun 1-3. Closed Jan 1, Good Fri, 1st Mon in
May, Dec 24-26. Adm fee

This historic building on the W side of
Kensington Gardens was one of the homes of
the British sovereign from 1689 to 1760 and
the birthplace of Queen Victoria (1819).
Originally Nottingham House, it was
purchased in 1689 by William III, who
suffered from asthma and disliked Whitehall
Palace for its proximity to the river. At that
time Kensington Palace was in the country
with Kensington Gardens forming a part of
the estate.

William commissioned Sir Christopher
Wren to enlarge the palace, and his work is
preserved today in the fine *S wing*, fronted
by a statue of the King. In the time of
George I the palace was further enlarged by
William Kent, and the State Apartments
(restored in 1973 and open to visitors) are
partly his work and partly Wren's. Most
interesting are the rooms where Victoria
lived as a princess, filled with her
mementoes, particularly the bedroom from
which she was summoned in 1837 in the
early hours of the morning to hear the news
of her accession.

Another recently restored building in the
palace is the elegant *Orangery*, which is
thought to be the work of Nicholas
Hawksmoor for Queen Anne (1704). With
the exception of the State Apartments the
palace is now given over to grace and favour
apartments and to relatives of the royal
family. It is at present the home of Princess
Margaret, Prince and Princess Michael of
Kent, and the London home of the Prince
and Princess of Wales.

Kenwood House
See *Museums & Galleries* p. 65

Kew Palace (The Dutch House) GL B2
Tube: Kew Gardens or boat from Westminster
Pier. Bus: 7, 27, 65, 90B. Apr-Sep, daily 11-5.30.
Adm fee

Set in the magnificent *Royal Botanic
Gardens* (p. 75) the Dutch House at Kew is
the last remaining of the three royal palaces
that once stood in the Gardens. (The other
two were demolished last century). It is also
the oldest, built in 1631 for a wealthy
merchant of Dutch parentage and only
becoming a royal palace under the
Hanoverian kings. It is a modest brick-built
house which now contains the relics of
George III and his family.

In the SW corner of the gardens stands
Queen Charlotte's Cottage, built for George
III's consort in 1772 as a summer-house and
picnic retreat. Upstairs are paintings by
George III's daughter, Princess Elizabeth.

Lambeth Palace J6
Lambeth Road SE1
Tube: Westminster then bus 3, 77, 159, 170. Bus:
10, 44, 149, 168, 507

Since the 12th c. this has been the official
home of the Archbishop of Canterbury. Like
the royal palaces it was sited on the river, for
easier communication. The buildings are
mainly of the 15th and 16th c., but there are
earlier and later parts. Most impressive is the
Gatehouse, with its twin towers, a fine
example of Tudor brickwork. The *Great
Hall*, rebuilt after destruction during
Cromwell's Commonwealth, retains a fine
hammerbeam roof and windows of
16th-17th-c. glass. This is the scene of the
Lambeth Conference of Anglican bishops; it
also houses a magnificent library of
illuminated manuscripts and early printed
books. The hall was seriously damaged again
in the last war, but carefully restored. Worse
damaged was the *Chapel* (c. 1230) which had
to be largely rebuilt and was rededicated in
1955. The crypt of this chapel (c.1200) is the
oldest part of the palace and retains its vault
and Purbeck marble pillars. The *Guard
Chamber*, rebuilt by Edward Blore (who also
built the residential part of the palace,
1828-33) retains its 14th-c. timber roof. Here
hang many fine historical portraits of
Archbishops.

Lancaster House G5
St James's Palace SW1
Tube and bus as Buckingham Palace. Easter-mid
Dec, Sat, Sun & Bank Hols, but often closed for
Government functions. Adm fee

Commissioned in 1825 for George III's
second son, the 'Grand Old' Duke of York,
this building – known then as 'York House'
– had two architects. Benjamin Wyatt built
the first two storeys. After the Duke of
York's death (1827) the building was taken
over and completed by one of his creditors,
the Marquess of Stafford (later the Duke of
Sutherland), who used Robert Smirke and

Sir Charles Barry (architect of the Houses of Parliament). Like much of Barry's decorative work in the Palace of Westminster, the interior here is extremely lavish, particularly the *Staircase Hall*, which rises to the full height of the building.

Stafford House, as it became known, was subsequently bought by the millionaire, the first Viscount Leverhulme, and renamed Lancaster House after his native county. He presented it to the nation and it is now used as a conference centre and for Government banquets.

Law Courts

See *Fleet Street & City Walk* p. 20

Lincoln's Inn WC2   J3

Tube: Chancery Lane. Bus: 8, 22, 25, 171, 501. *Chapel & Gardens* Mon-Fri 12-2.30. Closed Bank Hols. *Halls & Library* Apply in writing

The earliest record of this Inn was in 1422, when a school of lawyers was accommodated in a mansion of the Earl of Lincoln, in Chancery Lane. Before the establishment of the Law Courts in 1882 the Hall of this Inn was used as the Court of Chancery, and today is still the home of Chancery practitioners. Unlike Gray's Inn and the Temple, Lincoln's Inn escaped the worst of the bombing in World War II and most of its 17th-19th-c. buildings survived.

The Inn can be entered either from Chancery Lane or Lincoln's Inn Fields by a connecting road between the entrances. On the W is the neo-Tudor *New Hall*, built in 1843 to replace the old Hall which was at that time still being used as a court. Adjacent to it is the *Library*. To the S of the road is the 17th-c. *New Square* where Dickens served as a clerk. To the E, on the Chancery Lane side, are the Old Buildings which include the *Old Hall* (1491, restored 1928), in whose former court Dickens set the action of Jarndyce vs. Jarndyce in *Bleak House*, and the 17th-c. *Chapel* which has fine Flemish glass, restored after being shattered by a Zeppelin bomb in 1915. The poet John Donne, who laid the foundation stone of the Chapel, preached the first sermon here. The fine *Gatehouse* facing Chancery Lane, the oldest part of the existing Inn, was built in 1518. Names of famous Lincoln's Inn lawyers include Sir Thomas More, William Penn, Horace Walpole, William Pitt, Benjamin Disraeli and William Gladstone.

Mansion House

See *Fleet Street & City Walk* p. 22

Marble Arch W1   F4

Tube: Marble Arch. Bus: 2, 2B, 6, 7, 8, 12, 15, 16, 16A, 30, 36, 36B, 73, 74, 88, 137, 500, 616

Modelled on the Triumphal Arch of Constantine in Rome, this arch by John Nash (1828) was intended to be the main entrance to Buckingham Palace.

Unfortunately the opening proved too narrow for the State Coach and the arch was moved in 1851 to its present site at the W end of Oxford Street, where it stands on a traffic island.

Marble Hill House   GL B3

Richmond Road, Twickenham, Middlesex Tube: Richmond then bus 27, 90, 90B, 202, 270. Bus 33, 73. Sun-Thur 10-5 (Nov-Jan closes at 4)

Dating from 1724-9, Marble Hill is a perfect example of a Palladian villa. It was built by Roger Morris for Henrietta Howard, the mistress of George II. It later became the home of Mrs Fitzherbert, the secret wife of George IV. The symmetrical white stucco house of exceptional elegance stands in grounds designed by the poet Alexander Pope. The lovely rooms have period furniture.

Marlborough House and Queen's Chapel   H5

Pall Mall SW1

Tube and bus as Buckingham Palace. *House* Mon-Fri by prior arrangement with Administration Officer *Chapel* Mon-Fri 9-5 but currently closed for restoration

Built by Sir Christopher Wren for the Duke of Marlborough (1709-11) this later became the official residence of the Prince of Wales (1850). At this time the building was enlarged and became the centre of the pleasure-loving coterie, the 'Marlborough House Set' which was later to typify the Edwardian era. Inside, on the walls of the Great Saloon and staircase, is a remarkable series of paintings by Louis Laguerre, of Marlborough's most famous battles.

The last royal occupant of Marlborough House was Queen Mary, who died in 1953. It is now under Government ownership as the Commonwealth Centre.

In the grounds, and included in a tour of the house, is the **Queen's Chapel**. This was designed by Inigo Jones for Henrietta Maria, the Catholic queen of Charles I, and contains beautiful panelling and pews and an elaborate coffered ceiling.

Monument   M4

Fish Street Hill EC3

Tube: Monument. Bus: 8A, 10, 23, 27, 35, 40, 43, 44, 47, 48, 95, 133, 501, 513. Mon-Sat 9-5.40 (Apr-Sep) 9-3.40 (Oct-Mar), Sun 2-5.40 (May-Sep only). Closed Jan 1, Good Fri, Easter Mon, 1st Mon in May, Dec 24 & 25. Adm fee

Erected by Sir Christopher Wren in 1671-7 to commemorate the Great Fire of London, this monument is 202ft high and placed exactly 202ft E of the point where the fire was said to have broken out, in a baker's shop in Pudding Lane. The hollow column of Portland stone has an interior staircase leading to a platform at the top, with a fine view of the City and the river. The column is topped by a gilded flaming urn.

Nelson's Column H5
Trafalgar Square WC2
Tube: Charing Cross. Bus: 1, 3, 6, 9, 11, 12, 13, 15, 23, 24, 29, 53, 77, 77A, 88, 159, 170, 176

London's most famous monument stands as the centrepiece of Trafalgar Square, laid out by Sir Charles Barry to commemorate Admiral Lord Nelson's great victory over the French at Trafalgar, 1805. Designed by William Railton this monument was erected in 1840-3. The column of Devon granite over 167ft high is surmounted by a statue of Nelson by E. H. Bailey, over 17ft high. On the pedestal are bronze reliefs of scenes from Nelson's four most famous battles, cast from French cannon. The four bronze lions at the base are the work of Sir Edwin Landseer (1868). The base of the column is a traditional speaker's platform at rallies and demonstrations.

Old Bailey K3
(Central Criminal Court)
Old Bailey EC4
Tube: St Paul's. Bus: 55, 68, 77, 77A, 77C, 170, 172, 188. Admission when courts in session: Mon-Fri 10.15 & 1.45

A landmark of the London scene, whose dome is topped by the famous figure of Justice. Built in 1902-7, and restored after bomb damage, the Old Bailey stands on the site of Newgate Prison, which existed here from the 13th c. until 1902. This notorious prison was the scene of public hangings until 1868. It was visited by Elizabeth Fry, the prison reformer, who did much to improve conditions. A statue of Miss Fry (d. 1845) stands in the finely decorated hall.

Old Curiosity Shop J4
Portsmouth Street, Kingsway WC2
Tube: Holborn. Bus: 5, 68, 77A, 170, 172, 188, 239

This antique shop near Lincoln's Inn Fields, popularly identified with Charles Dickens' novel, is a fascinating survival of the 16th c.

Osterley Park House GL A2
Tube: Osterley. Bus: 91, 116, Green Line 704. Apr-Sep, Tue-Sun & Bank Hol Mon 2-6; Oct-Mar 12-4. Closed Jan 1, Good Fri, 1st Mon in May, Dec 24-26. Adm fee

Originally built by Sir Thomas Gresham, the richest merchant in Tudor England, Osterley was transformed in the 1760s to the designs of the great classical architect Robert Adam. Adam designed not only the rooms but also the furniture, fittings and even door

Buckingham Palace

handles. All his work survives, and with the chairs and tables arranged formally around the walls of each room, Osterley is a remarkable record of 18th-c. grandeur and taste. The park, ruined by the M4 motorway which slices through it, has a Greek temple, garden house and stable block.

Prince Henry's Room K4
17 Fleet Street EC4
Tube: Temple. Bus: 4, 6, 9, 11, 15, 171, 502, 513.
Mon-Fri 1.45-5, Sat 1.45-4.30

Over the gateway that leads into Inner Temple Lane, Prince Henry's Room is in one of the few London houses that was not destroyed in the Great Fire. The exterior has fine half-timbering and the interior oak panelling and a strap-work plaster ceiling. In the centre of the ceiling (early 17th-c.) is the *fleur-de-lis* and initials P. H. of Henry, Prince of Wales, son of James I. There is a permanent Samuel Pepys exhibition.

The Queen's House, Greenwich GL D2
Transport as for Royal Naval College. Tue-Sat 10-6, Sun 2-5.30 (5pm winter)

Designed in 1616 by Inigo Jones for James I's queen, this small palace was not completed for another 21 years when Charles I's wife Henrietta Maria used it. It was the first Palladian building to be erected in Britain, and the austere symmetrical white front must have appeared revolutionary at the time.

The palace was built over the Old Deptford Road and traffic continued to trundle through the building until the early 19th c., when the road was diverted and its route marked with the colonnades which connect the palace with the National Maritime Museum (p. 67). The palace is now part of the museum, but some of the rooms have period furnishings and paintings.

The Ranger's House, Greenwich GL D2
Transport as for Royal Naval College. Daily all year 10-5 (closed Nov-Jan). Closed Dec 24, 25 & Good Fri

A small Stuart house enlarged in 1753 by the 4th Earl of Chesterfield, an unhappy man whose chief solace was his house: 'my acre of ground here affords me more pleasure than kingdoms do kings.' Inside is the Suffolk Collection of Tudor and Stuart portraits, possibly the finest collection of early portraits in the country.

Royal Albert Hall and Albert Memorial
Kensington Gore SW7   D6/D5
Tube: South Kensington, Knightsbridge.
Bus: 9, 52, 73

Both the hall and the memorial, on the S side
of Hyde Park, were built in honour of Queen
Victoria's consort, Prince Albert (1819-61).
The hall, designed by Royal Engineer
Captain Francis Fowke, was completed in
1871. It has the form of a huge oval
amphitheatre, 273ft across and 155ft high,
roofed by an iron and glass dome. Around
the exterior below the dome is a terracotta
frieze depicting the Triumph of Art and
Science. The hall, which holds 8000 people,
is used for concerts (most notably the Sir
Henry Wood Promenade Concerts),
reunions, public meetings, boxing etc.
Visitors admitted (not during performances).

The **Memorial**, designed by Sir George
Gilbert Scott, was completed in 1876. It
epitomises the extravagent mid-Victorian
taste. Granite steps lead up to an ornate
tabernacle, in which the prince is seated,
holding the catalogue of his beloved project,
the Great Exhibition of 1851. Around the
pedestal are allegorical groups representing
the Working Man and a frieze of 178 figures
of poets, artists, composers and architects.

Royal Exchange
Cornhill EC3
Tube and bus as Bank of England. Closed to the
public during restoration

This building of 1842-4, with its imposing
Corinthian portico, is the third to stand on
the site. The original, built by Sir Thomas
Gresham (1565) as a commercial centre, was
burnt down in the Great Fire and its
successor destroyed by another fire in 1838.
The campanile, topped by Gresham's
grasshopper symbol, recalls the original bell
tower, used to summon the merchants.

Royal Mews
Buckingham Palace Road SW1   G6
Tube and bus as Buckingham Palace. Wed, Thur
2-4. Closed for ceremonial processions, Royal
Ascot week (Jun). Adm fee

Here are kept the royal coaches used for
ceremonial occasions, including the golden
State Coach used for coronations, the Irish
State Coach used for the State Opening of
Parliament and the glass State Coach used
for Royal Weddings. The royal horses are
stabled here.

Royal Naval College
Painted Hall and Chapel   GL D2
King William Walk, Greenwich SE10
British Rail: Greenwich, Maze Hill. River: from
Charing Cross, Westminster or Tower Pier. Tube:
Surrey Docks then bus 108B, 188. Bus: 53, 54,
75, 177, 180, 185. Daily 2.30-5 (not Mon). Closed
Good Fri, Dec 22-28

This noble group of classical buildings by
the Thames at Greenwich was begun in the
1660s, and continued from 1697 by Sir

Christopher Wren and others as a home for
disabled seamen (Greenwich Hospital). It
stands on the site of the old 15th-c.
Greenwich Palace (known also as Placentia),
a favourite residence of the Tudor monarchs.
The buildings consist of four separate
blocks, two of them with colonnades and
surmounting cupolas flanking the vista to
Inigo Jones' Queen's House. The SW block
contains the **Painted Hall** with magnificent
wall and ceiling paintings by Sir James
Thornhill (1708-20) and the SE block the
splendid **Chapel**. In 1873 the Hospital
became the Royal Naval College.

St James's Palace and Chapel Royal   G5
Pall Mall SW1
Tube and bus as Buckingham Palace. Closed to
public except for Chapel Royal (see below)

This historic palace was built by Henry VIII
1532-40 on the site of a leper hospital
dedicated to St James: hence the name. Of
this Tudor Palace only the four-storey
gatehouse facing up St James's Street and
the Chapel Royal survive. Soon after it was
built, the palace fell out of the king's favour:
the explanation of this might be in the royal
ciphers over the gateway. These are of the
king and his second wife Anne Boleyn, his
queen when the palace was begun but
subsequently executed on a charge of
adultery. Although many future kings and
queens were born here, St James's only
became the official metropolitan palace of
the sovereign in 1698, when Whitehall
Palace burned down. 140 years later (1837)
Buckingham Palace took over as the
sovereign's residence, but the tradition was
established and ambassadors to this country
are still accredited to the Court of St James.

The palace now contains grace and favour
apartments granted by the sovereign and is
the London home (York House) of the Duke
and Duchess of Kent. There is no public
access to the palace. The **Chapel Royal**,
approached by the Ambassador's Gate to the
W of the gatehouse is, however, open for
Sunday services in the winter. This chapel
has witnessed some stirring royal events,
among them Charles I's last service on the
morning of his execution and the wedding of
Queen Victoria. The coffered ceiling was
painted in 1540, probably by Hans Holbein
the Younger.

Somerset House   J4
Strand WC2
Tube: Temple, Embankment. Bus: 1, 4, 6, 9, 11,
13, 15, 55, 68, 77, 77A, 77C, 168, 170, 171, 172,
176, 188, 239, 513. Fine Rooms open for
occasional exhibitions

This huge building overlooking the river
near Waterloo Bridge (1776-86, architect Sir
William Chambers) stands on the site of the
16th c. palace built by Edward Seymour,
Duke of Somerset, uncle and Lord Protector
of Edward VI. After Somerset's execution in

1552, the palace was used as a 'dower palace' for English queens and in 1760 it passed to Charlotte, George III's consort. In 1776 the old palace was demolished and rebuilt by Chambers to accommodate the Royal Academy of Art and other learned bodies – George III having given the palace for public use in exchange for the formal title of residence to Buckingham House. In the 19th c. Somerset House became exclusively government offices, notably the Registry of Births, Marriages and Deaths. When this was moved (to St Catherine's House in Kingsway) the Search Rooms – used for researching family histories – were restored to their former elegance, and are now known as the Fine Rooms.

Stock Exchange   M4
Threadneedle Street EC2
Tube: Bank. Bus: as Bank of England. Mon-Fri 9.45-3.15 all year except Bank Hols. Free lecture and film at intervals 10-2.30

25,000 transactions, worth about £700 million, are made every day on the floor of the Stock Exchange. This is the largest financial market in the world, trading in stocks, shares and securities to a value of £400,000 million. But the visitor to the gallery will not see any money change hands. The 'brokers' buy from the 'jobbers' with a brief exchange of words and an entry in a notebook. The excellent short lecture and film explain the maze of activity. Although the building is modern (1973) with all the latest technology, dealings are clinched exactly as they were in coffee houses on the site in the 17th c.

Syon Park   GL B2
London Road, Brentford, Middlesex
British Rail: Syon Lane. Tube: Gunnersbury then bus 237, 267. Bus: 37, 117, 203, E2. Easter-Sep, Sun-Thur 12-5; Oct, Sun 12-5. Adm fee

Syon was built by Edward Seymour, Lord Protector Somerset, in the mid 16th c., and the shell of his house forms the present building. In the 18th c. the property passed to the Dukes of Northumberland, and in 1766 Robert Adam was engaged to transform Syon House. His attention to detail, including the furniture and gilded friezes of classical antiquities, makes this one of his greatest masterpieces. The grounds (the site of a bloody Saxon battle in 1016 and the Battle of Brentford in the Civil War (1642)) were landscaped by Capability Brown and contain rare shrubs and bushes. (See *Parks & Gardens* p. 75)

The Temple   K4
EC4
Tube: Temple, Aldwych. Bus: 4, 6, 9, 11, 15, 171, 502, 513 Mon-Fri 7am-8pm. The Embankment entrance never closes

Originally the headquarters in England of the Knights Templars of Jerusalem, the estate passed to the Crown when the order was suppressed (1312). The land was granted to the Knights Hospitallers of St John who in turn leased it to lawyers in the reign of Edward III. The Inner and Middle Temples have, together with Gray's Inn and Lincoln's Inn, remained the centre of legal life in this country ever since.

The Temple can be reached by Inner Temple Lane which opens onto Fleet Street with a narrow alley underneath Prince Henry's Room, (p. 55). The round *Temple Church* (p. 45) is in Church Court, the first of many such courts. Unfortunately the church, and most of the Temple buildings, were destroyed during the last war and have had to be rebuilt. In the SE corner of the court are the *Inner Temple Hall* (1952-5) and *Library* (1958). From Church Court, both Pump Court and Elm Court lead W to the Middle Temple. Fountain Court off Middle Temple Lane was immortalised by Dickens in *Martin Chuzzlewit*. Others who have lived or worked in the Temple include Sir Walter Raleigh, Edmund Burke, John Evelyn, Thomas de Quincey, Oliver Goldsmith and W. M. Thackeray. Charles Lamb, who also lived here, described it as 'the most elegant spot in the metropolis'.

The *Middle Temple Hall* (open Mon-Fri 10-12 and 3-4.30), built in 1572 with a magnificent double hammerbeam roof, was the scene of the first performance of *Twelfth Night* (1602) in which Shakespeare himself may have acted. The High Table, given by Sir Francis Drake, is made from timbers of the Golden Hind, (the first ship to circumnavigate the world). *Crown Office Row* runs E from the Hall and has views over the Temple Gardens stretching down to the Thames. *King's Bench Walk*, which runs N into *Old Mitre Court*, has some fine 17th-c. sets of chambers. From Old Mitre Court another narrow passage leads back to Fleet Street.

★ Tower of London   N4
Tower Hill EC3
Tube: Tower Hill. Bus: 23, 42, 78. Mar-Oct, Mon-Sat 9.30-5, Sun 2-5; Nov-Feb, Mon-Sat 9.30-4, closed Sun. Closed Jan 1, Good Fri, 1st Mon in May, Dec 24-26. Adm fee. Separate adm fee for *Jewel House* (closed Feb) and *Royal Fusiliers Museum*

For description and tour, see p. 29

York Watergate   J5
Victoria Embankment WC2
Tube: Charing Cross, Embankment. Bus: as Nelson's Column

In Victoria Embankment Gardens, 500ft from the river, this watergate is an interesting survival of York House, built in 1626-7 for the Duke of Buckingham. Its site marks the line of the original river bank before the building of the Embankment (1864-70).

Roman London

In 43AD the Romans invaded Britain,
driving its natives before them. Probably in
the same year a strategically important
bridge over the Thames was built, a little
downstream from today's London Bridge. A
fort, roads, quays and houses soon followed,
and *Londinium*, as it was called, became the
supply-base for the Roman legions. By
60AD it was the administrative capital of the
Roman province. A year later the city was
sacked and burnt by the rebellious Queen
Boadicea, but was soon restored and enjoyed
some three centuries of prosperous Roman
rule. This ended when the city fell to the
Saxons in the mid-5th c. Today little
remains of *Londinium*, though a temple and
parts of the walls and the fort have been
found. We also know of a rich palace by the
Thames at Cannon Street and a giant forum,
square in shape with sides of 182yds, which
lay on the area between Fenchurch Street
and Leadenhall Street.

Many of the most beautiful treasures of
Londinium are now on display in the *British
Museum* (p. 61) and the *Museum of London*
(p. 66).

Church of All Hallows by the Tower M4
Byward Street EC3
Tube: Tower Hill. Bus: 9, 42, 78

In the crypt (apply to the Verger for
admission) there are, beneath the Saxon
arches, two sections of red tessellated floor in
their original position. These probably date
from a 2nd c. Roman house. Also on show
are imported Samian pots, a model of
Roman London and several Roman
tombstones. (Open 9-6 every day)

Cripplegate Fort L3
Noble St, Museum of London, St Alphage
Gardens, EC2
Tube: St Paul's, Barbican. Bus: 4, 141, 279A, 502

The Romans built this large fort early in the
2nd c. Square in shape and some 12 acres in
size, it held a garrison of about 1500 men.
Remains of the W wall are preserved in
Noble Street, including the base of the
square corner tower. The wall can be
followed northwards through the gardens of
the Museum of London. At the NW corner,
the tall, largely medieval Cripplegate Bastion
stands majestically beside a modern lake,
together with remnants from the N wall of
the fort.

Another section of the fort wall is to be
found in St Alphage Gardens, off Wood
Street. Much is medieval and the brickwork
battlements are Tudor. From the stairs at
the E end, the wall is seen to be double: the
outer is the fort wall and the inner was added
when the fort became part of the city wall,
built in 200AD. (Viewable at all times)

*View of the Thames
from Victoria Tower*

London Stone M4
111 Cannon Street EC4
Tube: Bank, Cannon Street. Bus: 9, 18, 95, 149, 176A, 513

Embedded in the wall of a bank, opposite the railway station, is the broken-off tip of the mysterious pillar that stood in the road until 1742. It is now believed to have been part of the entrance to a great Roman palace that stretched some 420 yds down to the river. This building, with its grand state rooms, riverside gardens and pools, was probably the residence of the Governors of Britain. It is said that Cannon Street Station was built upon the 8ft-thick Roman walls, for even gunpowder could not shift them.

Roman Wall N4
Tower Hill and Cooper's Row EC3
Tube: Tower Hill. Bus: 9, 42, 78

Around 200AD the Romans enclosed 330 acres of city with about 2m of wall. It stood some 20ft high and was about 8ft thick; inside was a mound and outside a ditch. The stone, the equivalent of 5000 tipper-lorry loads, was brought by ship from quarries in Kent. The wall, many times built up and destroyed, survived until the 18th c.

Two splendid stretches are visible just N (in Cooper's Row) and S of Tower Hill tube station. Only the wall's lower portion, with regular stonework and red strengthening tiles, is Roman. Opposite the wall on Tower Hill is a copy of the tombstone of Julius Alpinus Classicianus, the chief imperial officer who protected the Britons against excessive repression by the Roman Governor after the defeat of Queen Boadicea. More remains of the City's Roman and medieval walls are visible within the *Tower of London* (p. 29) and in the garden of *All Hallows Church*, London Wall (p. 40). (The wall, apart from that in the Tower, is viewable at all times.)

Temple of Mithras L4
11 Queen Victoria Street EC4
Tube: Bank. Bus: 6, 8, 11, 15, 21, 22, 23, 25, 43, 76, 133, 149, 501, 502

The small temple was in use from the 1st to the 4th c. AD. The nave, apse and the pillar bases are clearly visible, as is the entrance threshold, worn by the tread of Roman worshippers. These reconstructed remains may be viewed at all times. Popular with the soldiers, Mithras was a sun-god of Persian origin. The temple boasted a wealth of fine marble statues: Mithras, Minerva, Bacchus, Mercury and others. The beautiful head of Mithras, with other treasures, is now on display in the *Museum of London* (p. 66).

Museums, Galleries & Homes of the Famous

Apsley House
See *Wellington Museum*

Baden-Powell House D6
Queen's Gate SW7
Tube: South Kensington, Gloucester Road. Bus: 49, 74. Daily 9-5. Closed Dec 22-Jan 2

Headquarters of the Scout Association and a memorial to its founder, Lord Baden-Powell. Mementoes of B-P and other exhibits tell the story of the Scout movement from 1907.

Battle of Britain Museum GL B1
Hendon NW9
Tube: Colindale. Bus: 79, 142. Mon-Sat 10-6, Sun 2-6. Closed Jan 1, Good Fri, 1st Mon in May, Dec 24-26. Adm fee

This newly-opened museum, an extension of the Royal Air Force Museum, commemorates the great air battle (Jul-Sep 1940) in which British pilots successfully defended the country from concerted Luftwaffe attacks. The collection includes World War II aircraft from both sides and a reconstructed RAF operations room.

Bear Gardens Museum L5
Bear Gardens, Bankside,
Southwark SE1
Tube: Cannon Street, London Bridge. Bus: 18, 70, 95, 149, 176A. Apr-Dec, Fri-Sun 10.30-5.30. Other days by appointment (Tel 928 6342). Closed Good Fri, Easter Sat, Dec 24-26. Adm fee

Converted 18th-c. warehouse on the site of the old Bear Baiting Ring and Hope Playhouse (where some of Shakespeare's plays were originally performed). The museum contains an Elizabethan Theatre exhibition, including scale models of Shakespeare's Globe, and a diorama of Southwark at the time of the Great Ice Fair on the Thames in the late 17th c. Upstairs is a small theatre used for occasional plays.

Bethnal Green Museum of Childhood GL C2
Cambridge Heath Road E2
Tube: Bethnal Green. Bus: 8, 8A, 106, 253. Mon-Thur, Sat 10-6; Sun 2.30-6. Closed Fri, Jan 1, Good Fri, 1st Mon in May, Dec 24-26.

Opened in 1872, this is a branch of the Victoria and Albert Museum. The building was, in fact, the original design for the South Kensington Museum (as the V & A was formerly known) with an iron and glass roof designed by Sir William Cubitt – an important example of the type of roof pioneered by Sir Joseph Paxton's 1851 Crystal Palace. Apart from the historic collection of dolls, dolls' houses, model theatres, etc. (see *Children's London* p. 76) there is a fine collection of 19th-c. English decorative art.

★ British Museum and **British Library**   H3
Great Russell Street WC1

Tube: Tottenham Court Road, Goodge Street,
Russell Square, Holborn. Bus: 68, 77A, 170, 188,
239 to Southampton Row; 7, 8, 19, 22, 25, 38, 55
to New Oxford Street; 14, 24, 29, 73, 134, 176 to
Great Russell Street. Mon-Sat 10-5, Sun 2.30-6.
Closed Jan 1, Good Fri, 1st Mon in May, Dec
24-26

The world's largest museum, designed by
Sir Robert and Sydney Smirke (1823-52).
The fine porticoed front was by Robert, the
Reading Room and dome by Sydney.
Founded in 1753, the museum was originally
in Montague House, Bloomsbury and was
formed from various collections including
the major bequest of Sir Hans Sloane
(d. 1753). To this was added the libraries of
George II and III, and since 1823 a copy of
every book printed, now about a mile of
books a year. The Museum is the principal
home of the **British Library**, though the
building of new premises is now being
undertaken at Euston.

The museum is on two floors. On the
ground floor (W wing) are the Egyptian,
Assyrian, Greek and Roman rooms. Exhibits
of unique interest include the *Rosetta Stone*
(195BC) inscribed with a decree in three
languages (Greek, demotic Egyptian and
Egyptian hieroglyphs) which gave scholars
the key to the Egyptian language; sculptures
from two of the Seven Ancient Wonders
(*Mausoleum of Halicarnassus, Temple of
Artemis*) and the famous *Elgin Marbles*, the
classical Greek sculptures from the
Parthenon, Athens, which were brought to
England in 1802-12 (Duveen Gallery). In the
E wing are the Printed Books and
Manuscripts, which include some of the
world's most precious literary and
documentary treasures, such as two versions
of the *Magna Carta* (1215) and the *Gutenberg
Bible* (*c*.1454). The upper floor has relics of
prehistoric, Roman and medieval Britain,
including the beautiful *Mildenhall Treasure*
of Roman silver and the relics from the
7th-c. *Sutton Hoo Ship Burial*. Also on this
floor are the Upper Egyptian Galleries and
the Greek and Roman Vase Rooms.

Two other sections of the British Museum
whose collections are housed in separate
buildings are the *Museum of Mankind* and
the *Natural History Museum*.

Bruce Castle Museum   GL C1
Lordship Lane N17

Tube: Seven Sisters, Wood Green then bus 123,
243. Tue-Fri 10-5, Sat 10-12.30 & 1.30-5. Closed
Sun, Mon & Bank Hols

On the ground floor of the former school run
by Britain's postal pioneer, Rowland Hill,
this museum presents a history of Britain's
postal services up to the introduction of the
penny post (1840). Upstairs is the museum
of the Middlesex Regiment.

Carlyle's House   E8
24 Cheyne Row, Chelsea SW3

Tube: Sloane Square then bus 11, 19, 22; South
Kensington then bus 45, 49. Bus: 39. Apr-end
Oct, Wed-Sat, Bank Hol Mon 11-5; Sun 2-5.
Closed other Bank Hols. Adm fee.

Thomas Carlyle, the 19th-c. philosopher and
historian, dubbed 'The Sage of Chelsea',
lived here from 1834-81. The house is
furnished modestly and is much as Carlyle
left it. Letters, books, family portraits and
many personal relics are on display. Carlyle's
statue stands in the gardens opposite Cheyne
Row, W of the bridge.

Commonwealth Institute   B6
Kensington High Street W8

Tube: High Street Kensington, Earls Court. Bus:
9, 27, 28, 31, 33, 49, 73. Mon-Sat 10-4.30, Sun
2-5. Closed Jan 1, Good Fri, 1st Mon in May, Dec
24-26.

This dramatic modern building (1962) set in
attractive gardens between Kensington High
Street and Holland Park is the exhibition
centre of the British Commonwealth. The
open-space interior, with several galleried
levels, offers glimpses of all the 35 Commonwealth countries, with dioramas and
displays of costume and handicrafts. The
centre includes a cinema, art gallery, library
and shop. (See *Children's London* p. 76)

Courtauld Institute Galleries   H2
Woburn Square WC1

Tube: Goodge Street, Euston Square, Russell
Square, Bus: 68, 77A, 170, 188, 239 to Woburn
Place; 14, 24, 29, 73, 176 to Gower Street or
Tottenham Court Road. Mon-Sat 10-5, Sun 2-5.
Closed Bank Hols, Good Fri, Dec 24-26.

The art collections bequeathed to London
University are exhibited in this impressive
small gallery. The Courtauld collection of
Impressionists and Post-Impressionists
includes such celebrated works as Cézanne's
Mt Ste-Victoire, Van Gogh's *Portrait of the
Artist with His Ear Cut Off*, Manet's *Bar at
the Folies-Bergère*, Renoir's *La Loge* and
other familiar paintings by Degas, Seurat,
Monet and Gauguin. Other benefactors were
Lord Lee (Renaissance works by Botticelli,
Rubens and others); Gambier-Parry (early
Italian works); Witt (Old Master drawings)
and Roger Fry (British and French paintings
of the late 19th and 20th c.).

Design Centre   H4
28 Haymarket SW1

Tube: Piccadilly Circus. Bus: 3, 6, 9, 12, 13, 14,
15, 19, 22, 23, 38, 53, 55, 88, 159, 500. Mon-Sat
9.30-5.30 (8 Wed-Thur). Closed Sun, Bank Hols,
Good Fri, Dec 25, 26

The best of British-designed products are
displayed here at the headquarters of the
Design Council. The exhibits are constantly
changed and updated, and some goods are
for sale. A photographic reference library
and design index are also available.

Dickens' House
J2

48 Doughty Street WC1

Tube: Russell Square. Bus: 5, 18, 19, 38, 45, 46, 55, 172. Mon-Sat 10-5. Closed Sun, Bank Hols & Christmas week. Adm fee

In this tall brick house Charles Dickens lived for two years from 1837. It is the only one of his London residences to have survived. Here he wrote *Oliver Twist, Nicholas Nickleby* and parts of *The Pickwick Papers* and *Barnaby Rudge*. The Dickens' Trust turned the building into a museum in 1924. It contains illustrations, portraits, letters, many of Dickens' personal belongings, and the largest library relating to Dickens in the world. The basement contains a reproduction of the 'Dingley Dell' kitchen, made famous in *The Pickwick Papers*.

Dr Johnson's House
K4

17 Gough Square EC4

Tube: Blackfriars. Bus: 4, 6, 9, 11, 15, 502, 513. May-Sep, Mon-Sat 11-5.30; Oct-Apr, Mon-Sat 11-5. Closed Sun & Bank Hols. Adm fee

This delightful building, the home of Dr Johnson from 1749 to 1759, was chosen for its long, well-illuminated garret. Here he and a team of six scribes worked for eight years on his great *Dictionary*, published in 1755. One of the first edition is on show. Apart from the attic, striking features of the house include the staircase and surrounding panelling. The small rooms on each floor contain 18th-c. furniture, some of it originally used by Johnson himself, and prints, letters and other personal items.

Dulwich Picture Gallery
GL C3

College Road SE21

British Rail: West Dulwich. Tube: Brixton then bus 3 to Thurlow Park Road. Bus: 37, P4 to Dulwich Village, 12, 78, 176, 176A, 185 to Dulwich Library. Tue-Sat 10-1 & 2-5, Sun 2-5. Closed Mon, Jan 1, Good Fri, Dec 24-28. Adm fee

London's first public art gallery, opened in 1814, was designed by Sir John Soane. It is best known for its collection of Dutch masters (Rembrandt, Vermeer, Cuyp etc.) and 17th-18th-c. British artists (Hogarth, Gainsborough, Reynolds, etc.).

Fenton House
See *Historic Buildings* p. 48

Geffrye Museum
N1

Kingsland Road E2

British Rail: Dalston. Tube: Liverpool Street then bus 22, 22A, 48, 149; Old Street then bus 243. Bus: 22, 67, 149, 243. Tue-Sat 10-5, Sun 2-5, Bank Hol Mon 10-5. Closed Mon, Jan 1, Good Fri, Dec 24-26.

Housed in attractive Ironmongers' Almshouses (1715) built by a former Lord Mayor of London and master ironmonger, Sir Robert Geffrye, this collection of furniture and objects from London's past is superbly arranged in a series of room-sets of different periods from 1600 to the 1930s.

Trafalgar Square
Inset: Piccadilly Circus

Geological Museum D6
(next to Science Museum)
Exhibition Road SW7
Tube and bus as Science Museum. Mon-Sat 10-6,
Sun 2.30-6. Closed Jan 1, Good Fri, 1st Mon in
May, Dec 24-26.

The appeal of this museum is not confined to
the student. Anyone with an interest in
geology and mineralogy will be stimulated
by the excellent displays, notably 'The Story
of the Earth' (ground floor) and the special
exhibits on the Regional Geology of Britain
and the search for North Sea Oil. Most
celebrated exhibit is a rock from the moon.
An excellent reference library is open to
visitors.

Guildhall Art Gallery and
Reference Library
See *Historic Buildings* p. 49

Hayward Gallery J5
South Bank SE1
Tube: Waterloo, Embankment. Bus: 1, 4, 5, 68,
70, 76, 149, 168A, 171, 176, 177, 188, 239, 501,
502, 507, 513. Mon-Thur 10-8, Fri-Sat 10-6, Sun
12-6. Closed between exhibitions, Jan 1, Good
Fri, 1st Mon in May, Dec 24-28. Adm fee

Part of the South Bank Arts Centre. Opened
in 1968 and run by the Arts Council, this
Gallery has two levels, with external
sculpture courts. Major art and cultural
exhibitions.

HMS Belfast M5
Symons Wharf, Vine Lane SE1
Tube: London Bridge, Tower Hill then ferry from
Tower Pier (summer daily, winter Sat-Sun). Bus:
23, 42, 47, 70, 78, 188. Daily 11-5.50 (4.30 in
winter). Last admission ½ hr before closing.
Closed Jan 1, Good Fri, 1st Mon in May, Dec
24-26. Adm fee

Permanently moored naval museum in
Britain's largest battle cruiser. 11,500 tons,
built in 1938, *HMS Belfast* took part in the
Battle of the River Plate (1941) and the
sinking of the *Scharnhorst* at North Cape
(1943). Access to most decks of the ship,
which is preserved with reconstructions of
life below deck.

Historic Ships Collection N5
St Katharine's Dock
Tube: Tower Hill. Bus: 9, 42, 67, 78. Apr-Sep,
daily 10-5; Oct-Mar, daily 10-4. Closed Jan 1, Dec
24 & 25. Adm fee

This collection of seven ships, all of which
are open for visitors to clamber aboard,
shows the evolution from sail to steam and
the way ships were adapted for specific
purposes.

In addition to a Thames tug, a lightship
and the last surviving top-sail schooner, you
can see Captain Robert F. Scott and Sir
Ernest Shackleton's research ship *RRS
Discovery*, which spent two years stranded in
solid ice in the Antarctic at the beginning of
this century.

Hogarth's House GL B2
Hogarth Lane, Chiswick W4
Tube: Hammersmith then bus 290. Apr-Sep,
Mon-Sat 11-6, Sun 2-6; Oct-Mar, Mon-Sat (closed
Tue) 11-4, Sun 2-6. Closed Bank Hols. Adm fee

William Hogarth, the 18th-c. artist, chose
this as his country villa in 1749 and remained
here until 1764, shortly before his death. His
body was carried back to Chiswick and is
buried in the churchyard of St Nicholas,
near the house.

The house itself provides a typical
example of Queen Anne architecture: it is a
red-brick building with three storeys. The
small rooms are lined with examples of
Hogarth's satirical works – *The Rake's
Progress* and *Mariage à la Mode*, for instance.
Apart from these prints, there are also one or
two items of 18th-c. furniture on display.

Horniman Museum GL C3
London Road, Forest Hill, SE23
British Rail: Forest Hill. Bus: 12, 12A, 63, 176,
176A, 185, P4. Mon-Sat 10.30-6, Sun 2-6. Closed
Dec 24-26.

Housed in an *art nouveau* building by C. H.
Townsend, this is the personal collection of
F. J. Horniman, an MP and tea merchant.
The emphasis is ethnographic – dance masks
and totems, primitive tools and musical
instruments from all over the world. There is
also a natural history section where a
working beehive can be seen (during the
summer months only). Fine ethnographical
library.

Imperial War Museum K6
Lambeth Road SE1
Tube: Lambeth North, Elephant & Castle. Bus: 1,
3, 10, 12, 44, 45, 53, 63, 68, 109, 141, 155, 159,
171, 172, 176, 177, 184, 188. Mon-Sat 10-5.50,
Sun 2-5.50. Closed Jan 1, Good Fri, 1st Mon in
May, Dec 24-26

The building which houses Britain's major
war museum was completed in the year of
Waterloo (1815) for a quite different
purpose: the Bethlem Hospital for the
Insane (Bedlam). The dome and portico
were added by Sydney Smirke in 1846. The
war museum, founded in 1917, was moved
here in 1936 from the Imperial Institute in
South Kensington.

The exhibits cover all military campaigns
involving British and Commonwealth forces
since August 1914. The majority are from
the two World Wars and include aircraft,
both enemy and allied; submarines, mines
and torpedoes; tanks and field guns;
numerous models and dioramas of trench
warfare, Normandy landings, etc.; and
uniforms, equipment and medals. The
museum's picture galleries show a selection
of 10,000 paintings, drawings and prints,
most of them by official war artists. There
are three libraries: books, photographs and
films. Special temporary exhibitions are also
arranged.

Institute of Contemporary Arts (ICA) H5
Nash House, The Mall SW1

Tube: Charing Cross, Piccadilly Circus. Bus: 1, 3, 6, 9, 11, 12, 13, 15, 23, 24, 29, 53, 77, 77A, 88, 159, 168, 170, 172, 176, 500. Tue-Sun 12-9. Closed Mon, Dec 25, 26. Membership, plus adm fee for exhibitions

This porticoed Nash building is an unlikely exterior for the activities of the ICA, devoted as it is to the latest ideas in contemporary art. The centre includes an art gallery, cinema and theatre (occasional productions only).

Keats House See Hampstead map
Keats Grove, Hampstead NW3

Tube: Belsize Park, Hampstead. Bus: 24, 46, 187, 268, C11. Mon-Sat 10-6, Sun, Bank Hol Mon 10-1 & 2-6. Sun & Bank Hols 2-5

Keats House was originally two semi-detached houses with a communal garden. In one half lived Charles Brown, who in 1818 invited Keats to live with him, and in the other, the Brawne family. The youngest daughter, Fanny, became Keats' fiancée. Here he lived until his departure for Rome, where he died in 1821. Converted in 1838, this peaceful Regency house has been restored and re-decorated. It contains a fine collection of manuscripts and letters as well as books owned by Keats at school and medical college. Adjacent to the house is the Keats' Memorial Library, containing a vast amount of material pertaining to Keats and his contemporaries.

Kenwood House See Hampstead map
Hampstead Lane NW3

Tube: Archway or Golders Green then bus 210. Green Line: 734. Apr-Sep, daily 10-7; Oct & Feb-Mar 10-5; Nov-Jan 10-4. Closed Good Fri, Dec 24, 25.

One of London's most distinctive art collections is housed in this beautiful Georgian mansion overlooking Hampstead Heath. Rebuilt 1767-9 by Robert Adam for the Earl of Mansfield, Kenwood was bequeathed to the nation by the Earl of Iveagh (1927) together with his collection of paintings. The house has 18th-c. furnishings. Adam designed the *Library*, with its elegant plasterwork and delightful pastel colour scheme. The paintings are mainly from the English, Dutch and Flemish Schools and include Vermeer's *Guitar Player* and Rembrandt's *Self-Portrait in Old Age*. The masters of English portraiture, Sir Joshua Reynolds, Thomas Gainsborough and others, are also represented.

The grounds of Kenwood, sweeping down to the tree-shrouded lake, make an attractive setting for the open-air concerts in the summer.

Kensington Palace State Apartments
See *Historic Buildings* p. 52

Kew Bridge Engines GL B2
(Living Steam Museum)
Green Dragon Lane, Brentford.

British Rail: Kew Bridge. Tube: Gunnersbury then bus 27, 65, 237, 267. Sat-Sun, Bank Hols 11-5. Adm fee

This museum of steam engines is housed in the Kew Bridge Pumping Station. Electric pumps have now taken over, but the Kew Bridge Engines Trust have restored a number of the old beam engines to full working order. Model steam engines and the original Victorian workshops are also on display.

Leighton House B6
12 Holland Park Road W14

Tube: High Street Kensington. Bus: 9, 27, 28, 31, 33, 49, 73. Mon-Sat 11-5. Closed Sun, Bank Hols, Good Fri, Dec 25 & 26.

This unusual and splendid building, now a centre for Victorian studies and a gallery of Victorian paintings, drawings and sculpture, was the inspiration of Lord Leighton, a former President of the Royal Academy who lived here until his death in 1896. The original and exotic taste of the owner are best seen in the beautiful *Arabian Hall* decorated with its fountain court and Oriental tile decoration. The art and craftsmanship of the period are seen in the tilework of William de Morgan and the pictures of Sir Edward Burne-Jones, Sir Lawrence Alma-Tadema, Sir John Everett Millais and others. An adjoining wing houses the *British Theatre Museum*, opened in 1963.

London Transport Museum J4
(Transport Museum)
Covent Garden WC2

Tube: Covent Garden, Leicester Square. Bus: 1, 6, 9, 11, 13, 15, 23, 24, 29, 77, 77A, 170, 176. Daily 10-6. Closed Dec 25 & 26. Adm fee

The history of London's public transport over the last 200 years is shown in Sir William Cubitt's restored Flower Market. The exhibits include horse-buses, trams, trolley-buses, and the steam locomotive used on the first underground railway. Working exhibits and audio-visual displays add to the interest. (See *Children's London*, p. 76)

Madame Tussaud's F3
Marylebone NW1

Tube: Baker Street. Bus: 1, 2B, 13, 18, 27, 30, 74, 113, 159, 176. Daily 10-5.30 (6pm Apr-Sep). Closed Dec 25 & 26. Adm fee (Royal ticket includes entrance to Planetarium)

This world-famous waxworks exhibition was brought from Paris to London in 1802 by Marie Tussaud, a Swiss modeller. The waxwork gallery of the famous and notorious, living and dead, is continually updated. Reconstructions of historical events are a popular feature. In the basement is the chilling Chamber of Horrors. (See *Children's London* p. 76)

Museum of Artillery GL D2
(Rotunda Museum)
Woolwich Common SE18
British Rail: Woolwich Dockyard. Tube: New
Cross or New Cross Gate then bus 53. Bus: 54,
75. Mon-Fri 12-4, Sat-Sun 1-4 (5pm Apr-Oct).
Closed Jan 1, Good Fri, Dec 25 & 26

Part of the Royal Artillery barracks at
Woolwich, the Rotunda (John Nash, 1814)
houses weaponry of various periods used by
the artillery, including cannon, howitzers,
mortars and machine-guns.

Museum of Garden History J6
St Mary-at-Lambeth,
Lambeth Palace Road SE1
Tube: Westminster then bus 3, 77, 159, 170. Bus:
10, 44, 149, 168A, 507. Mon-Fri 11-3, Sun
10.30-5. Closed Sat, 2nd Sun in Dec – 1st Sun in
Mar

St Mary-at-Lambeth, closed in 1972, is
being restored by the Tradescant Trust as
the first Museum of Garden History. In the
churchyard, restyled as a 17th c. garden, are
the tombs of Admiral Bligh of the Bounty
and the two John Tradescants, gardeners to
Charles I and Henrietta Maria.

Museum of London L3
London Wall EC2
Tube: Barbican, St Paul's, Moorgate. Bus: 4, 141,
279A, 502 or 8, 22, 25, 501 to St Paul's. Tue-Sat
10-6, Sun 2-6. Closed Mon, Bank Hols, Dec 24-27

This new museum, in an exciting new
building at the end of London Wall, was
opened in 1976. It combines the former
London Museum and the Guildhall
Museum, and tells the story of the capital
from its origins to the present.

Illustrated panels of the prehistoric
settlements begin the story, with
accompanying objects from the Stone,
Bronze and Iron Ages. Roman London
shows the commercial and strategic
development of the city, with pottery, tools
and the remains of a wooden ship; also a
mosaic pavement and finds from the Temple
of Mithras. (A section of the Roman city wall
is visible from the museum.) The Saxon and
Viking antiquities include a formidable array
of weapons, and the medieval, Tudor and
Stuart periods show armour, costumes and
everyday objects. A model of London
Bridge, and an audio-visual display of the
Great Fire of 1666 are great attractions.
Reconstructed interiors of later periods offer
the contrast of a cell of Newgate prison and a
fashionable Victorian drawing-room. More
recent exhibits include a Woolworth's
counter, fully stocked, and an Art Deco lift
of the '30s from Selfridges. Wartime London
is graphically reconstructed.

The museum's most famous exhibit is the
majestic *Lord Mayor's State Coach*, removed
from the museum once a year in November
to carry the newly-elected Lord Mayor to his
inauguration.

Museum of Mankind G4
6 Burlington Gardens W1
Tube: Piccadilly Circus, Green Park. Bus: 9, 14,
19, 22, 25, 38, 55. Mon-Sat 10-5, Sun 2.30-6.
Closed Jan 1, Good Fri, 1st Mon in May, Dec
24-26

The Ethnography Department of the British
Museum has its own permanent exhibition,
in the street behind the Royal Academy.
Displayed here are exhibits from tribal
societies, many of them displayed in
specially reconstructed habitats. Exhibits
include shadow puppets from Java, elaborate
ceremonial costumes from Hawaii, African
and Oceanic carvings, and a beautiful Aztec
skull of rock crystal from Mexico. Special
exhibitions are mounted periodically with
linking film shows.

Museum of the Order of St John K3
St John's Gate, St John's Lane,
Clerkenwell EC1
Tube: Farringdon. Bus: 5, 55, 243, 277, 279. Tue,
Fri, Sat 10-6, other days by appointment (Tel 253
6644)

The 16th-c. gatehouse of the now vanished
priory of the Order of St John of Jerusalem
houses a museum of .ne Order.

National Army Museum F8
Royal Hospital Road SW3
Tube: Sloane Square. Bus: 11, 39, 137 to Royal
Hospital Road. Mon-Sat 10-5.30, Sun 2-5.30.
Closed Jan 1, Good Fri, 1st Mon in May, Dec
24-28

The story of the British Army, from the
Battle of Bosworth (1485) to 1914 is
displayed in this modern, well-designed
museum. Based on the collection of the
Military Academy at Sandhurst, it includes a
comprehensive range of weapons, uniforms
and decorations. Models of battlefields,
recorded soldiers' ditties and a simulated
shooting gallery are special attractions.
Military paintings include portraits by
Reynolds, Romney and Lawrence.

★ National Gallery H4
Trafalgar Square WC2
Tube: Charing Cross, Leicester Square,
Embankment. Bus: 1, 3, 6, 9, 11, 12, 13, 15, 23,
24, 29, 53, 77, 77A, 88, 159, 168, 170, 172, 176,
500. Mon-Sat 10-6, Sun 2-6. Closed Jan 1, Good
Fri, 1st Mon in May, Dec 24-26

The national collection of paintings, one of
the world's finest, is housed in a domed
neo-classical building (1838) on the N side of
Trafalgar Square. The terrace, beneath the
Grecian portico, offers a unique view down
Whitehall to the Houses of Parliament.

The collection covers all schools and
periods, but is particularly strong on the
Dutch and Flemish and the Italian
15th-16th c. The British School is better
represented at the Tate, as are the 20th-c.
Moderns: the gallery has, however, a fine
collection of French Impressionists.

A short selection of the works in this gallery gives an idea of the impressive range: Van Eyck's *Marriage of the Arnolfini*, Botticelli's *Mars and Venus*, Leonardo da Vinci's *Virgin of the Rocks*, Holbein's *The Ambassadors*, Piero della Francesca's *Baptism of Christ*, Titian's *Death of Actaeon*, Rubens' *Judgement of Paris*, El Greco's *Agony in the Garden*, Velázquez' *Rokeby Venus*, Rembrandt's *Adoration of the Shepherds*, Cézanne's *Les Grandes Baigneuses*, Van Gogh's *Landscape with Cypress Trees* and many others. Such is the wealth of works that it is probably better to confine a visit to a single period or school if there is an opportunity for a return visit.

National Maritime Museum   GL D2
Greenwich SE10
British Rail: Maze Hill. Tube: Surrey Docks then bus 108B, 188. Bus: 53, 54, 75, 177, 180, 185. Tue-Fri 10-6 (5 in winter), Sat 10-6, Sun 2-5.30 (5 in winter)

The Queen's House, built by Inigo Jones for the consorts of James I and Charles I, with its two colonnaded wings, is the Greenwich home of Britain's premier museum of the sea and ships. Galleries here and in the Royal Observatory cover many different aspects of maritime history in paintings and engravings, mementoes of great sea battles and captains, navigational instruments and charts. The *West Wing*, which covers the Napoleonic Wars, includes a special section on Nelson, with the uniform worn by him at the Battle of Trafalgar; the *East Wing* concludes the history of naval warfare with World War II. The new Neptune Hall contains examples of actual vessels, including a paddle tug, a Thames pleasure launch and the *Barge House*, the state barge of Mary II (1689). Among the many fine paintings in the museum's galleries of seascapes, naval battles and portraits, are works by the Van de Veldes, Turner, Hogarth, Reynolds and Gainsborough. The print room and library offer valuable sources for naval historians.

The *Royal Observatory*, on the hill on the far side of Greenwich Park, was designed by Sir Christopher Wren in 1675 (see p. 101).

National Portrait Gallery   H4
St Martin's Place WC2
Tube and bus as National Gallery. Mon-Fri 10-5, Sat 10-6, Sun 2-6. Closed Jan 1, Good Fri, 1st Mon in May, Dec 24-26

Portraits of the famous, chosen for their subject matter but naturally including examples of many masters such as Holbein, van Dyck, Gainsborough, Reynolds and Sargent. Recent portraits of Prince Charles and the Princess of Wales by Brian Organ have attracted popular interest. Visitors will find it fascinating to trace the likeness in famous families through the generations.

Regular special exhibitions are mounted in the gallery, and there is now further display space in Carlton House Terrace overlooking the Mall.

National Postal Museum   L3
King Edward Street EC1
Tube: St Paul's. Bus: 4, 8, 22, 25, 141, 501, 502. Mon-Thur 10-4.30, Fri 10-4. Closed Sat, Sun, Bank Hols, Dec 24-26

One of the world's most comprehensive stamp collections, incorporating the Phillips collection of 19th-c. British stamps and the Post Office collections of British and foreign stamps.

★ Natural History Museum   D6
Cromwell Road, South Kensington SW7
Tube and bus as Science Museum. Mon-Sat 10-6, Sun 2.30-6. Closed Jan 1, Good Fri, 1st Mon in May, Dec 24-26

Officially The British Museum (Natural History), this is one of London's most popular museums, housed in a majestic and ornate Victorian building in the Romanesque style (Alfred Waterhouse). The scientific collections of Sir Hans Sloane (1753) and the botanical collection of Sir Joseph Banks (1820) form the basis of this splendid display of the world's plants, minerals and wildlife.

Most compelling are the fossilized skeletons of the great dinosaurs which dominate the Central Hall and the adjacent Fossil Collection. Another monster – extant – is the Blue Whale: a skeleton of one is in the Whale Hall, with a life-size model (91ft long) suspending from the ceiling.

Separate galleries are devoted to Birds, Fish, Crustacea, Reptiles, Insects and Mammals, and exhibits include the extinct Dodo of Mauritius and the 'living fossil', the Coelecanth. The Rowland Ward Pavilion, in the Mammal Gallery, shows a marvellous range of African Mammals in their natural habitat. In the Mineral Gallery is a gigantic Iron Meteorite weighing 3½ tons, found in 1854 near Melbourne.

Special displays explain the story of evolution, and there is a Hall of Human Biology in which new interpretative techniques – push-button machines, illuminated models, etc. illustrate the mechanism of our own bodies (an instructive section for children).

Overlord Embroidery   L3
Whitbread Brewery, Chiswell Street EC1
Tube: Moorgate, Barbican. Bus: 21, 43, 76, 104, 141, 214, 271. Mon-Sat 10-5, Sun 2-6. Closed Jan 1, Dec 24-26. Adm fee

Sponsored by Whitbread Brewery, this unique tapestry commemorates 'Operation Overlord', the Normandy landings of June 6, 1944. The largest work of its kind in the world, it has 34 panels, and is 272ft in length.

Photographers' Gallery H4
5 & 8 Great Newport Street WC2
Tube: Leicester Square. Bus: 1, 14, 19, 22, 24, 29, 38, 176. Mon-Sat 11-7, Sun 12-6. Closed Bank Hols, Good Fri, Dec 24-27

This gallery specialises in photographic exhibitions; they change every 1-2 months and cover a wide range of themes from historical to one-man shows. Prints, art books, magazines and postcards are on sale and there is an extensive reference library.

Pollock's Toy Museum
See *Children's London* p. 76

Public Record Office Museum K4
Chancery Lane WC2
Tube: Chancery Lane, Temple. Bus: 4, 6, 9, 11, 15, 23, 171, 502, 513. Mon-Fri 1-4, Closed Sat, Sun, Bank Hols, Good Fri, Dec 24-28

The Public Record Office, main repository for the country's archives and legal records, contains a small museum where a selection of historic documents is on view to the public. Most notable is the *Domesday Book*, in two volumes. This survey of England, ordered by William the Conqueror (1086), has been reproduced in facsimile for the public to consult. Other fascinating documents include Guy Fawkes' confession, the *Magna Carta*, Royal Autographs from the Black Prince onwards, William Shakespeare's will and the log-book of Lord Nelson's *Victory* at Trafalgar.

Queen's Gallery G6
Buckingham Palace Road SW1
Tube: Victoria. Bus: 2, 2B, 10, 11, 16, 24, 25, 29, 36, 36A, 36B, 38, 39, 52, 55, 70, 76, 149, 185, 500, 507. Tue-Sat, Bank Hols 11-5, Sun 1-5. Closed Mon, between exhibitions, Good Fri, Dec 23-25. Adm fee

The only access for the public to Buckingham Palace is offered by a visit to this small Royal Gallery, once the Palace chapel, which presents a changing exhibition of rarely-seen treasures from the Royal Collection.

Royal Academy of Arts G4
(Burlington House)
Piccadilly W1
Tube: Piccadilly Circus, Green Park. Bus: 9, 14, 19, 22, 25, 38, 55. Daily 10-6. Closed Good Fri, Dec 24-27. Adm fee

Founded in 1768 under royal patronage, the RA moved to its present quarters in Burlington House in 1869. The building, originally the work of the third Earl of Burlington (1715), was greatly enlarged and embellished in the ensuing 150 years, with the exhibition galleries added by Sydney Smirke in 1869.

The RA comprises 50 Academicians and 25 Associates. The Academicians select works of art submitted by the public for the annual Summer Exhibition (May-Jul/Aug), which has been held regularly since 1769.

Only about 1500 works are shown out of 11,000 submitted. The private rooms contain diploma works by the Academicians, historical relics of the Academy, and the famous 'Michaelangelo Tondo', the only sculpture by the artist in Britain. Special exhibitions are also mounted in the galleries.

Royal Air Force Museum GL B1
Hendon NW9
Tube: Colindale. Bus: 79, 142. Mon-Sat 10-6, Sun 2-6. Closed Jan 1, Good Fri, 1st Mon in May, Dec 24-26

Two of the original hangars of the old Hendon Aerodrome are used to display the historic aircraft of Britain's principal museum of aviation. The arrangement is chronological, from the World War I Sopwith Camel to modern jet fighters. The early history of flight, from the balloon to the biplane, is shown in a wide range of exhibits.

The history of the RAF is imaginatively reconstructed in sets depicting the early Royal Flying Corps workshops, a WAAF mess, etc. A gallery of flying heroes is of great interest and there is a splendid library and art gallery, as well as one of the best museum shops. Nearby is the *Battle of Britain Museum*.

Royal Hospital Museum F8
Royal Hospital Road SW3
Tube: Sloane Square. Bus: 11, 39, 137. Mon-Sat 10-12 & 2-4, Sun 2-4. Closed Good Fri, Easter Sun, 1st Mon in May, Dec 24-26

The Chelsea Pensioners' Regimental Museum, part of the Royal Hospital. Medals, uniforms and weapons, prints and drawings going back to the foundation of the hospital in the 17th c. (See *Chelsea Royal Hospital*, p. 47)

Royal Observatory
See *National Maritime Museum*

St Bride's Crypt Museum
See *Churches* p. 41

★ **Science Museum** D6
Exhibition Road SW7
Tube: South Kensington. Bus: 14, 30, 45, 49, 74. Mon-Sat 10-6, Sun 2.30-6. Closed Jan 1, Good Fri, 1st Mon in May, Dec 24-26

One of London's most popular museums, for those of all ages who want to know 'how it works'. Established in 1857, the museum is continually expanding, as befits an exhibition of the developing world of technology and industry.

The historical side begins with the Industrial Revolution and includes models of James Watt's first steam engines. Electric power is represented by a reproduction of Michael Faraday's original experiments in electricity generation, and models of power stations. Road and rail transport are demonstrated by working models and vehicles, and a major section of the museum is devoted to air and sea navigation. The space section gives pride of place to the original Apollo 10 space capsule and to a 'moon buggy'. On a more down-to-earth level is the Domestic Science Gallery, where the workings of everyday objects are explained. (See *Children's London* p. 76)

Serpentine Gallery D5
Kensington Gardens W2
Tube: Lancaster Gate, Knightsbridge. Bus: 9, 52, 73. Daily 10-6. Closed between exhibitions. Good Fri, Dec 24-26

Between the Serpentine and Alexandra Gate, this gallery, run by the Arts Council, specialises in exhibitions by contemporary artists.

Sir John Soane's Museum J3
13 Lincoln's Inn Fields, WC2
Tube: Holborn. Bus: 5, 8, 22, 25, 55, 68, 77A, 77C, 170, 172, 188, 239, 501. Tue-Sat 10-5. Closed Sun, Mon, Bank Hols, Good Fri, Dec 24-26

Three adjoining houses on the N side of the square (Nos 12-14) built by Sir John Soane, the architect and collector. No 13, in which he lived until his death, was adapted by him as a museum for his collection of antiquities and paintings, and it looks much as it did in his lifetime. Soane's ingenuity in maximising the limited space of the interior is shown in his use of mirrors and wall screens. The varied collection includes antique marbles and a number of paintings by famous British artists including William Hogarth's series *The Rake's Progress* and *The Election*. There are over 20,000 architectural drawings, including Soane's own prolific work. In the basement is the huge alabaster sarcophagus of Seti 1, King of Egypt *c*.1370BC.

★ Tate Gallery H7
Millbank SW1
Tube: Pimlico. Bus: 77A, 88. Mon-Sat 10-6, Sun 2-6. Closed Jan 1, Good Fri, 1st Mon in May, Dec 24-26

After the National Gallery, this is London's most important art collection and the home of the national collection of British art. It is also the country's premier gallery of modern art. The gallery was built due to the generosity of Sir Henry Tate, the sugar refiner, and opened in 1897. The building, a classical work of Sidney R. J. Smith, has been added to over the years and a new extension was opened in 1978. The British paintings cover all the major artists from the 16th-20th c., with particularly fine collections of Gainsborough, Hogarth, Reynolds, Stubbs, Blake, Constable, Lawrence and Turner. The Pre-Raphaelites are well represented, as are the later Victorians and Edwardians (Whistler, Watts, Sargent and Sickert). Contemporary British artists include Nicholson and Sutherland.

The modern section of the gallery is

international, ranging from the French Impressionists to American abstract expressionists. Modern sculpture includes works by Rodin, Epstein and Moore. Special exhibitions are a regular feature.

★ Victoria & Albert Museum D6
Cromwell Road SW7
Tube and bus as Science Museum. Mon-Thur, Sat 10-5.50, Sun 2.30-5.50. Closed Fri, Jan 1, Good Fri, 1st Mon in May, Dec 24-26

This complex and comprehensive museum of fine and applied art is one of the country's greatest public collections. It was started as a Museum of Manufactures by Prince Albert and Sir Henry Cole, with a nucleus of objects from the Great Exhibition (1851). The present building of Sir Aston Webb, with its fine Renaissance façade, an extension of earlier buildings, was opened in 1909. The scale of the collection is such as to demand a selective approach, and exhibits are therefore divided into Primary Collections, in which works are displayed by date, style or nationality, and Study Collections, in which works are related by type – ceramics, textiles, metalwork etc. Ornamental Art is a major theme and there are splendid displays of costumes, armour, jewellery, musical instruments and many other artefacts from all the world. Special exhibitions are devoted to individual artists, crafts or movements.

In an annexe is the newly-opened *Boilerhouse Project*. Regular exhibitions on the history, theory and practice of design.

Wallace Collection F3
Manchester Square W1
Tube: Bond Street. Bus: 1, 2, 2B, 13, 30, 74, 113, 159 to Portman Square; 6, 7, 8, 12, 15, 16A, 73, 88, 137, 500 to Oxford Street, Selfridges. Mon-Sat 10-5, Sun 2-5. Closed Jan 1, Good Fri, 1st Mon in May, Dec 24-26

This splendid collection, beautifully arranged in an 18th-c. mansion (Hertford House) off Oxford Street, is the creation of the 4th Marquess of Hertford and his son, Sir Richard Wallace. By perceptive purchases, father and son used their wealth to amass one of the finest collections of works of art in the country, bequeathed to the nation by Wallace's widow in 1897. Lord Hertford, who lived mostly in Paris, was a specialist in 18th-c. French art, and the collection includes splendid works by Watteau, Boucher and Fragonard. French furniture of the period, and fine Sèvres porcelain are also on view. Other purchases embraced the Dutch, Flemish and Spanish Schools: here the most famous paintings are Franz Hals' *The Laughing Cavalier* and Rembrandt's portrait of *The Artist's Son Titus*. Sir Richard Wallace's additions to the collection were mainly the splendid array of European arms and armour and objects of Renaissance art: bronzes, enamels and Italian majolica.

Wesley's House & Museum M2
47 City Road EC1
Tube: Old Street. Bus: 5, 43, 55, 76, 104, 141,
143, 214, 271. Mon-Sat 10-4, Sun after 11am
service. Closed Bank Hols, Good Fri, Dec 24-26

This 18th c. building was the home of John
Wesley, the founder of Methodism, for the
last years of his life (1779-91). It now
contains a collection of Wesleyana. Next
door is Wesley's Chapel (the 'Cathedral of
Methodism') opened in 1778. Wesley's tomb
lies behind the Chapel. The crypt has a
library of 5000 books on the history of
Methodism.

Wellington Museum F5
Apsley House, 149 Piccadilly W1
Tube: Hyde Park Corner. Bus: 2, 2B, 9, 14, 16,
16A, 19, 22, 25, 30, 36, 36B, 38, 52, 73, 74, 137.
Tue-Thu, Sat 10-6; Sun 2.30-6. Closed Bank Hols

This house was for many years the first
Duke of Wellington's permanent London
home. It was designed by Robert Adam in
1768. It now contains a host of personal
possessions, from swords and snuff-boxes to
candelabras and a fine collection of
porcelain. There are also valuable paintings
by European masters (Goya, Correggio,
Velazquez, Rubens), some of which were
taken as booty after the Battle of Vitoria and
then donated to the Duke. The grandiose
Waterloo Gallery, added by Benjamin Wyatt
in 1829, was where banquets were held
annually to celebrate the famous battle. On
the original dining table is a highly ornate
Portuguese dinner service and a 26ft-long
silver centrepiece, both presents from the
Prince Regent of Portugal. The museum also
contains various busts of Wellington and an
impressive marble statue of Napoleon.

Whitechapel Art Gallery GL C2
80 Whitechapel High Street E1
Tube: Aldgate East. Bus: 5, 10, 15, 23, 25, 40, 56,
67, 253. Sun-Fri 11-6 during exhibitions. Closed
Jan 1, Good Fri, Easter Mon, Bank Hols, Dec
24-26. Closed in 1984 for renovation

The East End art gallery, offering three or
four exhbitions per year of modern and
contemporary art.

William Morris Gallery GL D1
Lloyd Park, Forest Road E17
Tube: Walthamstow Central. Bus: 34, 55, 69,
123, 275, 276, 278. Tue-Sat 10-1, 2-5; 1st Sun in
month 10-12, 2-5. Closed Bank Hols

This fine Georgian house, where William
Morris spent his youth, has now been
converted into an art gallery exhibiting work
by Morris' circle and containing furniture,
tapestries, stained glass, wallpapers, letters
and manuscripts by Morris himself. There is
also the Brangwyn Gift – a collection of
19th-20th c. paintings, drawings and
sculpture.

Streets, Squares & Colourful Areas

Barbican EC2 L3
The Barbican Estate was built by the City of
London as the final phase in the post-war
redevelopment scheme in the St
Paul's/London Wall area. The complex
includes residential blocks and the
impressive new Barbican Arts Centre, home
of the London Symphony Orchestra, the
Royal Shakespeare Company and the
Guildhall School of Music and Drama.

Bayswater W2 C4
This cosmopolitan area near Paddington
Station is full of hotels and bed-sits, with a
changing multi-national population that
ensures a varied range of food-shops and
restaurants, particularly in its main street,
Queensway (which also has an ice-rink). The
Bayswater Road is especially lively on
Sundays, when artists display paintings on
the Hyde Park railings.

Berkeley Square W1 G4
One of Mayfair's most fashionable squares.
(See *Mayfair Walk* p. 33)

Belgravia SW1 F6
Stuccoed Regency mansions, elegant squares
(notably Belgrave Square) and crescents
characterise this distinctly aristocratic
residential quarter. Disraeli's uncle, George
Basevi, along with Thomas Cubitt was
responsible for this development dating from
1827. Today, as well as being residential, it
is also the seat of foreign embassies and
various professional societies.

Bloomsbury WC1 H3
The home of the British Museum and the
heart of the University of London, the area
boasts intellectual connections, including
'The Bloomsbury Group' who lived here in
the first half of the century. Squares
dominate the area – in particular,
Bloomsbury Square, laid out in the 17th c.
by the Earl of Southampton.

Bond Street W1 G4
In the heart of Mayfair, this high-class,
fashionable street contains art galleries,
boutiques and jewellers. (See *Mayfair Walk*
p. 33 and *Shops & Markets* p. 82)

Camden Town NW1 G1
This area comprises a diverse mixture of well
preserved 18th-c. houses around Regent's
Park and shabby, decaying property in the
part bordering on Kentish Town. Regent's
Canal flows through the area (see *London's
Waterways* p. 86) and at Camden Lock arts
and crafts flourish: at the weekend a lively
market is held here (p. 83). Greek-Cypriot
tavernas abound, on and off the High Street.

Carnaby Street W1   G4

In the 60s this street, with its boutiques and psychedelic paving, was the essence of 'Swinging London'.

Charing Cross Road WC2   H4

Street marking the E border of Soho, running down to Trafalgar Square. Famous for its bookshops – new and second-hand.

Chelsea SW3   E7

A chic, fashionable quarter, dominated by the names of Cadogan and Sloane, who between them once owned the entire area. Most of Chelsea was laid out in the 1770s – Cadogan Square is typical, with its red brick houses. Sloane Square is today the home of the Royal Court Theatre, famous for its contemporary plays, and the department store Peter Jones. The Royal Hospital by the river, built by Sir Christopher Wren in 1682, is the home of veteran and invalid soldiers, who wear a traditional uniform of red-frock coats and caps. Cheyne Walk consists of elegant 18th-c. houses. King's Road, with its outlandish boutiques, has become a stage for the latest fashions.

City of London

See *City Walk* p. 20

Covent Garden WC1   J4

The 'piazza' was the first square to be built in London. It dates from the 17th c. and was partly designed by Inigo Jones, who was also responsible for the Church of St Paul's in the square. The site was formerly a garden belonging to the monks of Westminster Abbey. Today the 'piazza' is a fashionable show-case for specialist shops. Crafts proliferate in the area. The Royal Opera House, originally built in 1732 but twice destroyed by fire, dates as it now stands from 1856. It is the principal seat of opera and ballet in London.

Earls Court SW5   C7

This is a cosmopolitan area, dubbed at one time 'Kangaroo Valley' on account of its many Australians. Brimming with bedsitters and dubious looking hotels, the area focuses on the Earl's Court Road, teeming with food shops, restaurants and 'bucket shops'. The famous Exhibition Hall was opened in 1937 and acts as host to a diverse range of events from rock concerts to the famous Cruft's dog show.

Fleet Street EC4   K4

The hub of the newspaper industry. (See *City Walk* p. 20)

Grosvenor Square W1   F4

Dominated by the US Embassy, built by Eero Saarinen in 1960, this square also has a statue of Franklin D. Roosevelt in the gardens at its centre. (See *Mayfair Walk* p.34)

Hampstead and **Highgate** NW3 and N6

See p. 35

Islington N1   K1

Once a village outside of London, this area became fashionable and prosperous in the 18th and 19th c. It is growing fashionable again as the Regency squares and terraced houses are painstakingly restored. Islington Green preserves some village atmosphere, while Camden Passage contains countless antique stalls and is interwoven with other narrow lanes. Canonbury Square typifies early 19th-c. Islington in its layout. There is also a street market in Chapel Market (see *Shops & Markets* p. 83).

Kensington High Street W8   C6

Becoming increasingly cosmopolitan, this bustling high street in the Royal Borough of Kensington used to be noted for its elegant department stores. Sadly these have now diminished but the area is still popular with tourists. Nearby is Holland Park, formerly the grounds of a Jacobean manor. (See *Shops & Markets* p. 82 and *Parks* p. 75)

Leicester Square W1   H4

Famous for entertainments, with its cinemas, cabarets and dancing, this square was named after the 2nd Earl of Leicester who built a house close by in 1637. It was laid out in 1665 and converted into a public garden in 1874. It contains statues of William Shakespeare and Charlie Chaplin and busts of other famous people (Isaac Newton and William Hogarth, for example). In the NE corner stands the church of Notre Dame de France. After damage during the war, it was re-built in 1955 and now contains a small mural by Jean Cocteau.

Lincoln's Inn Fields   J3

One of London's largest garden squares – they are in fact gardens, laid out by Inigo Jones in 1618. They are a great favourite with 'City gents' who congregate here at lunchtime to stroll amongst the plane trees and tennis courts. On the N side of the square at No 13, is *Sir John Soane's Museum* (see p. 69). Lincoln's Inn (see p. 53), one of the four Inns of Court, lies to the SE.

Marylebone W1   F3

The name derives from 'St Mary on the Bourne', meaning 'a stream' (the Tyburn). The area was laid out in the 18th c. and became a popular residential area with fine streets, squares and terraces. Today's Euston, Pentonville and Marylebone roads were once known communally as New Road, a type of by-pass linking Paddington to Islington. Baker Street is famous as the home of the fictitious detective, Sherlock Holmes, while nearby Manchester Square contains Hertford House and the Wallace Collection (see *Museums* p. 69).

The Mall SW1   H5

This broad avenue, sweeping up to Buckingham Palace, forms an impressive backcloth for royal pageants. (See *Westminster Walk* p. 16)

Mayfair   F4

An expensive, fashionable area, though many former mansions are now offices. (See *Mayfair Walk* p. 32)

Oxford Street W1   F4

The most popular street for shopping in London. (See *Shops & Markets* p. 82)

Paddington W2   D3

Once a village and still retaining a green, though it is barely recognisable as such, this was a popular residential quarter in the 19th c. It declined in the years following, but is now rising again, notably in the area known as 'Little Venice'– around the starting point of the Regent's Canal (see *London's Waterways* p. 86).

Pall Mall SW1   H5

The origins of the name lie in the French words 'paille maille', a game similar to croquet introduced in Charles II's time. This broad, distinguished street is today noted for its exclusive clubs. It extends from the Haymarket to St James's Street – a very fashionable area, and contains some fine examples of 19th-c. architecture by Sir Charles Barry and John Nash.

Park Lane W1   F5

Flanking Hyde Park, for many years this street was one of the most opulent in London. Amongst its residents were Benjamin Disraeli and R. B. Sheridan. Today the mansions have nearly all gone: in their stead are prestigious hotels (The Hilton, for example, which towers 300 ft. over the park) and night clubs such as the Playboy Club.

Parliament Square SW1   H6

Dating from the mid 19th c., this square was designed to give a garden approach to the Houses of Parliament. (See *Westminster Walk* p. 13)

Piccadilly W1   H4

A select shopping street running from Piccadilly Circus – 'the hub of the universe' – to Hyde Park Corner. (See *Mayfair Walk* p. 32 and *Shops & Markets* p. 82)

Regent Street W1   G4

Laid out in the early 19th-c. by John Nash, this street has some of London's most exclusive stores. (See *Shops & Markets* p. 82)

Shaftesbury Avenue W1   H4

The heart of Theatreland, including theatres such as the Lyric, where Eleanora Duse made her stage debut in 1893.

Shepherd Market W1   G5

Chic, self-contained 'village' with wine bars and restaurants. (See *Mayfair Walk* p. 33)

Soho W1   H4

Full of character. It is perhaps best known as London's 'red light' district and comprises various nefarious entertainments from blue movies to strip clubs. It is also full of excellent restaurants, and in the area around Gerrard Street, otherwise known as China Town, Chinese restaurants proliferate. There are also some first class delicatessens, and Berwick Street Market. Soho Square, laid out in the 17th c., has a lovely garden at its centre. (See *Shops & Markets* p. 83)

South Kensington SW7   D7

A great cultural and scientific area, with no less than four important museums (the V & A, Natural History, Geological and Science Museums) all centred on the Exhibition Road, a site purchased from the proceeds of the Great Exhibition of 1851. The Royal Albert Hall, built 1867-71, is a striking oval amphitheatre, famous for its Promenade Concerts (founded 1895 by Sir Henry Wood). The area is also the home of Imperial College, part of the University of London.

Stepney E1   GL D2

Lying in the heart of the East End and bordering on dockland, this area was once considered a large den of iniquity. The Highway was full of seamen's taverns, while smugglers lurked in nooks such as *The Prospect of Whitby* (a 16th-c. inn, still standing). The view of the Thames from here inspired both Whistler and Turner. Today, however, much of the area's character has been lost in new development.

Strand WC2   J4

Originally skirting the banks of the Thames, which has since receded, this street has many theatres, shops and hotels.

Trafalgar Square WC2   H5

Nelson's Column towers over the square, populated with pigeons and sightseers. (See *Westminster Walk* p. 13).

Whitechapel E1   GL C2

Many Jewish traders and craftsmen settled here in the 19th c. following the persecution of the Jews in Russia. Although few tourists venture this far east, interest in the area is stimulated by one particularly infamous resident: Jack the Ripper, who in 1888 claimed a number of victims here. In the High Street is the Whitechapel Art Gallery.

Whitehall SW1   H5

A street lined with government buildings and the home of the Cenotaph, where the famous Poppy Day Memorial Service is held. (See *Westminster Walk* p. 13)

Parks, Gardens & Wildlife

With no less than 80 parks, London is the greenest capital in Europe. The origins of these parks are diverse. Some were common land, some the gardens of the nobility, some royal hunting grounds and others resulted from the Blitz of 1940-41.

Wildlife can be seen in most of London's parks, whether it be deer roaming free in Richmond Park or pandas in their enclosure in Regent's Park, the home of London Zoo. Botanical gardens range from Kew, with its great variety of exotic flora, to the more domestic Queen Mary's Garden in Regent's Park.

ROYAL PARKS

Green Park
See *St James's Park*

Greenwich Park SE10　　　　　　GL D2
British Rail: Maze Hill. River: from Charing Cross, Tower or Westminster Pier. Bus: 53, 54, 75, 180, 185

200 acres combining ornate flower beds, neat avenues and natural woodland glens, harbouring herds of deer. The park affords a striking view over London, as well as containing *The Queen's House*, begun in 1616 by Inigo Jones, the impressive *Royal Naval College*, and the former *Royal Observatory*. This is also the home of the Meridian Line, denoting zero longitude (hence the phrase 'Greenwich Mean Time'). Other attractions are a bird sanctuary, tennis courts and a children's play area. (See *Excursions* p. 101)

Hampton Court Park and Bushy Park
Teddington, Middlesex　　　　　　GL A3
British Rail: Hampton Court. River: from Westminster Pier. Bus: 111, 131, 152, 201, 211, 215, 216, 267. Green Line 715, 716, 718, 725, 726

These two parks are divided by Hampton Court Road: *Hampton Court Park* with its lawns, flower gardens and famous maze; *Bushy Park* with its grazing deer and cattle and carp-filled ponds. Of note in the latter is the mile-long avenue of chestnut trees, planted in 1699 and a stunning spectacle in the spring. (See *Excursions* p. 102)

Hyde Park W1　　　　　　　　　　E5
Tube: Hyde Park Corner, Marble Arch, Queensway. Bus: 2, 2B, 9, 14, 16, 16A, 19, 22, 25, 30, 36, 36B, 38, 52, 73, 74, 137

Originally part of the manor of Hyde, this park was bought by Henry VIII in 1536 and became one of his hunting grounds. It was opened to the public in the 17th c. and became a highly fashionable area for walking and riding. In the 18th c., however, the park became the haunt of highwaymen, footpads and duellists – this despite the fact that the Tyburn Gallows were close by. Queen Caroline, George II's consort, created the

Serpentine in 1730; it is now open for fishing, boating and swimming. *Rotten Row* (the name derives from *la route du roi* – 'the king's road') is a special track for riding. To the NE, near Marble Arch, is *Speaker's Corner* where, every Sunday morning, orators come to air their views. Here, it is said, Karl Marx came to listen, to improve his English. The Great Exhibition was held here in 1851.

Kensington Gardens W8　　　　　　C5
Tube: Kensington High Street, Lancaster Gate, Queensway. Bus: 9, 12, 27, 33, 49, 52, 73, 88

These elegant gardens, adjacent to Hyde Park, were originally the private grounds of William III's *Kensington Palace* – a lovely building re-designed by Sir Christopher Wren, and famous for its Orangery and Sunken Garden (see *Historic Buildings* p. 52). The playground, with its *Elfin Oak* carved with pixies, and the statue of *Peter Pan* beside the *Long Water* (a pond formed at the request of George II's Queen Caroline) make the gardens popular with children. Peter Pan's creator, J. M. Barrie, lived close by and regularly used to walk here. The tree-lined *Broad Walk* leads to the *Round Pond*, popular with model boat enthusiasts. *Flower Walk*, with its blooms and birdlife, leads to the *Albert Memorial*. 175ft high, this statue, erected by Queen Victoria, shows her husband, Prince Albert, holding the catalogue of the Great Exhibition of 1851 which he helped to instigate (see *Historic Buildings* p. 56). Nearby is the *Serpentine Gallery*, where exhibitions and concerts are held in the summer.

Regent's Park and Primrose Hill NW1　　F1
Tube: Baker Street, Regent's Park, Great Portland Street, Camden Town. Bus: 1, 2, 2B, 3, 13, 18, 27, 30, 53, 74, 113, 137, 159, 176

Once part of Henry VIII's hunting forest, this park was laid out for the Prince Regent in 1812 and named in his honour. It was planned that the prince should have a country villa here, and at the same time Nash built Regent Street to connect the park with Carlton House, the prince's London home. The park is surrounded by a carriage-way, the *Outer Circle*, lined with elegant Regency houses, also designed by Nash (completed, with further designs by Decimus Burton, in 1827). This road joins the *Inner Circle* which encloses a lovely rose garden (*Queen Mary's Garden*) and the *Open Air Theatre* (see *Theatres* p. 99), where Shakespeare plays are performed in the summer. The park also has a yachting and boating lake, playing fields and tennis courts, the Regent's Canal, Bedford College (part of London University) and a mosque – the first to be built in London. It is also the home of *London Zoo* (p. 75). *Primrose Hill*, N of the park, offers one of the finest panoramas of London.

73

Richmond Park   GL B3
Surrey
Tube: Richmond then bus 65, 71; Putney Bridge
then bus 85. Bus: 33, 37, 72, 73

Originally a royal hunting ground, laid out
by Henry VII, Richmond Park today spans
2470 acres and contains herds of red and
fallow deer. It is the largest of the royal parks
and is mainly grassland, interspersed with
gardens, plantations, golf courses and ponds
for fishing. There are facilities for most
sports from football and cricket to polo.
White Lodge, once George II's hunting box,
is now the home of the Royal School of
Ballet.

St James's Park and **Green Park** SW1 H5/G5
Tube: St James's Park, Charing Cross, Green
Park, Hyde Park Corner. Bus: 2, 2B, 9, 14, 16, 16A
19, 22, 25, 26, 30, 36, 36B, 38, 52, 73, 74, 137

One of London's most attractive parks, this
was originally an area of marshland. Henry
VIII drained *St James's* for hunting, and
Charles II had it laid out to continental
designs. John Nash then remodelled and
embellished the park with a lake and exotic
trees. To the N lies the Mall which sweeps
up to Buckingham Palace; to the S and W
are Birdcage Walk and Horse Guards. The
lake has an island which provides a sanctuary
for a large cross-section of fowl, from ducks
to pelicans. *Green Park*, an extension of St
James's, consists of vast stretches of grass.
To the S is Constitution Hill, w'.ere Charles
II used to take his 'constitutional' and where
three attempts were made on the life of
Queen Victoria.

OTHER PARKS

Alexandra Palace and **Park** N22   GL C1
Tube: Wood Green then bus W3; Finsbury Park
then bus W2, W3, W7

Crowning Muswell Hill, this park offers fine
views over London and the Home Counties.
At the summit is Alexandra Palace, from
which the first TV programme was
transmitted in 1936. Used for concerts and
exhibitions, the Palace was recently damaged
by fire and has been replaced by a temporary
building. Recreational facilities in the park
include an artificial ski-slope (Oct-Mar),
boating lake and children's zoo (Easter-Sep).

Battersea Park SW11   GL C2
Tube: Sloane Square then bus 137; South
Kensington then bus 49. Bus: 19, 39, 44, 170,
249, 295

The park stands flanking the Thames on
what was once marshland. For many years
the park's claim to fame was its funfair, but
this was closed in 1975. It is, however, an
attractive park with good facilities for sports,
a picturesque boating lake, a sub-tropical
garden, sculptures by Henry Moore and a
children's zoo (Easter-Sep). The park is also
the site of the popular Easter Parade.

Blackheath SE3   GL D3
British Rail: Blackheath. Bus: 53, 54, 75, 89, 108,
108B, 192

Historically famous as the spot where Wat
Tyler rallied his forces in 1381 during the
Peasant's Revolt, Blackheath is also the site
of a beacon used in 1588 to warn of the
approach of the Spanish Armada. As well as
the fair held every summer Bank Holiday,
there is soccer, cricket and boating on the
Prince of Wales pond. Elegant 18th- and
19th-c. houses surround the heath.

Crystal Palace SE19   GL C3
British Rail: Crystal Palace. Tube: Brixton then bus
2B, 3. Bus: 12, 12A, 63, 108B, 122, 137, 154, 157,
227, 249

The park once housed the Crystal Palace of
the Great Exhibition of 1851 – an enormous
structure of glass and iron, later destroyed
by fire. The grounds now contain a boating
lake, modern sculptures and life-size replicas
of dinosaurs, the latter on the islands in the
boating lake. There is a children's zoo
(Easter-Sep), with domestic animals, caged
birds and penguins, and a magnificent
National Sports Centre with a stadium seating
12,000 (see *Sport & Recreation* p. 81).

Dulwich Park SE21   GL C3
British Rail: West Dulwich. Tube: Brixton then
bus 3. Bus: 12, 37, 78, 176, 176A, 185, P4

Covering 72 acres, this park is noted for its
spectacular array of rhododendrons and
azaleas. The lake boasts a variety of wildfowl
and there is an aviary, nature trail, playing
fields, tennis courts and putting green.

Epping Forest   GL D1
Essex
Tube: Loughton, Theydon Bois, Epping,
Walthamstow Central then British Rail to
Chingford. Bus: 10, 20, 20A, 69, 102, 121, 167,
179, 191, 235, 242, 247, 254

The remains of the ancient forest of
Waltham, Epping Forest stretches from
Epping to Chingford. It is easy to get lost in
these 5800 acres of dense woodland,
comprising oak, beech, birch and holly.
Elizabeth I hunted here and her hunting
lodge at Chingford is now a *Forest Museum*.
Boats are for hire on Connaught Water,
while at Chingford there is golf. The
facilities for riding are good, and funfairs are
held on Wanstead Flats and Chingford
Plain.

Hampstead Heath NW3   GL C1
British Rail: Hampstead Heath, Gospel Oak. Tube:
Hampstead, Golders Green. Bus 24, 46, 187, 210,
268, C11

800 acres of wild, sandy heathland with
green hills, wooded dells, shaded lakes,
situated only 4m from Charing Cross. The
Heath contains a wealth of flora and fauna
and is interlaced with paths. Attractions
include the beautifully landscaped grounds

of *Kenwood House* (see *Museums* p. 65),
Parliament Hill (perfect for kite-flying and
grass-skiing), the *Bathing Ponds* (one for
women, one for men and one for mixed
bathing), *Golders Hill Park* with its various
animal enclosures and *Hampstead Fair*, held
every summer near the Vale of Health. Busy
at weekends, but often quiet during the
week, the Heath is popular with riders,
joggers, walkers and fishermen.

Holland Park W8   B6
Tube: Holland Park. Bus: 9, 12, 27, 28, 31, 33, 49,
73, 88

Once the private grounds of Holland House,
a Jacobean manor owned by the Earl of
Holland, the building was severely damaged
during World War II and has been partly
restored as a youth hostel. The atmosphere
here is tranquil, with peacocks strutting on
the lawns. There is a lovely 19th-c. *Dutch
garden* and an *Orangery*, used for exhibitions
of arts and crafts. The N side is mostly
woodlands. In summer there is an open-air
theatre. Many beautiful and exotic birds and
flowers may be seen in the park.

Lee Valley Park E15
See *Children's London* p. 77

Syon Park   GL B2
London Road, Brentford, Middlesex
British Rail: Syon Lane. Tube: Hammersmith then
bus 267; Gunnersbury then bus 237, 267. Bus:
37, 117, 203, E2. Gardens daily 10-6 (dusk
Nov-Feb), closed Dec 25 & 26. Adm fee

The Duke of Northumberland opened both
the house (see *Historic Buildings* p. 57) and
grounds to the public in 1969. The park was
laid out in the 18th c. by Capability Brown,
the famous landscape gardener. It provides
an elegant backcloth for the *Great
Conservatory* which contains an aquarium
and aviary (Easter-Oct) where exotic birds
fly free. Another glasshouse contains a
beautiful live butterfly collection (*The
London Butterfly House* p. 77). There is a
6-acre rose garden and a garden centre.

Waterlow Park N6   GL C1
Tube: Archway. Bus. 143, 210, 271, C11

Close to the village of Highgate, this
secluded park contains gently sloping
gardens, several ponds, an aviary and an
open-air theatre. In the grounds stands
Lauderdale House (p. 37).

Wimbledon Common and **Putney Heath**
SW19   GL B3
Tube: Putney Bridge then bus 39, 74, 85, 85A, 93,
Wimbledon then bus 93. Bus: 28, 72, 168

1000 acres of natural heathland and woods,
broken up with lakes on which model boats
are sailed. Reputedly, this commonland was
once infested with highwaymen who preyed
on the Portsmouth Road. Today there are
numerous bridleways, a golf course and, in
the centre of the common, a 19th-c. *windmill*.

BOTANIC GARDENS

Chelsea Physic Garden   8E
Royal Hospital Road, Chelsea SW3
Tube: Sloane Square. Bus: 9, 11, 39, 137.
Easter-Oct, Wed & Sun 2-5. Also 1st Mon in May,
Chelsea Flower Show week, Spring & Summer
Bank Hol 2-5. Adm fee

Founded in the late 17th c., this delightful
botanic garden with its 5000 plant species is
devoted to the cultivation of drug plants for
research and education. Newly opened to the
public, it has rock and herb gardens and
homeopathic plants.

★ **Kew Gardens**   GL B2
Surrey
British Rail: Richmond. River: from Westminster
Pier. Tube: Kew Gardens. Bus: 15, 27, 65, 90B.
Closed Bank Hols. Adm fee

Founded in 1759 by Princess Augusta,
mother of George III, the Royal Botanic
Gardens are the most famous in the world
and play a crucial role in the field of
botanical research. The beautiful grounds
contain over 45,000 different trees, shrubs
and plants. As well as the herbarium with
7 million specimens, there are many
hot-houses containing beautiful plants from
orchids to tropical ferns. The grounds are
lovely, with paths, temples, grottoes and
lakes, and are the home of the tallest flagpole
in the world (a Douglas Fir, 225ft tall) and a
Chinese Pagoda built by Sir William
Chambers in 1761. *The Palm House* (1848,
Decimus Burton) is one of the masterpieces
of mid-Victorian engineering and has the feel
of the jungle. There is also an excellent
reference library, three small botanical
museums and the *Dutch House* (see *Kew
Palace* p. 52) where King George III lived.
(See *Excursions* p. 102)

WILDLIFE

★ **London Zoo**
Regent's Park NW1   F1
Tube: Camden Town, Baker Street then bus 74.
Bus: 3, 53, 74, Green Line 735. Mar-Oct, daily 9-6,
Nov-Feb 10-4. Closed Dec 25. Adm fee (half price
on 1st Sat of each month)

A great favourite with visitors to London,
the zoo attracts over 1 million people a year –
no surprise as it boasts around 6000 animals,
some rarely seen in captivity. Most popular
are the penguins, sea-lions and the giant
pandas. The layout is imaginative: there is a
walk-through aviary designed by Lord
Snowdon, while, on the Mappin terraces,
bears and other animals live in relative
freedom, unrestricted by cages. Other
special attractions are the Elephant and
Rhino House, the Small Mammal House
with simulated nocturnal conditions, and the
magnificent new Lion Terraces. Aquarium,
Reptile House, and Children's Zoo also
popular. Good to visit at feeding times.

Children's London

With its museums, parks, theatres and cinemas, special exhibitions and numerous other activities, London has endless entertainments for children, with always something extra at weekends. Listed below are the places that children will find interesting throughout the year, but to find out about any extra events – particularly during the school holidays – one of the following should be phoned:

What's On A guide to entertainment and events by the British Tourist Authority. Tel 246 8041
Stewpot's Children's London. Tel 246 8007
Capital Kidsline School holidays only, 10-5. Tel 222 8070

Bethnal Green Museum of Childhood
Cambridge Heath Road E2 GL C2
Tube, bus and opening times p. 61
The Victoria and Albert Museum's collection of dolls and dolls' houses, displays of games, jigsaw puzzles, model soldiers and toys, fascinate both children and collectors. There are regular special exhibitions, and a permanent collection of wedding dresses and Spitalfields' silk. A special feature is the exhibition of model theatres.

BBC Ticket Unit
Broadcasting House, London W1A 4WW
Free tickets are available to watch BBC TV and radio shows. Minimum age for radio shows is 8, for TV shows 10. Details of coming attractions from the above address (enclose a stamped addressed envelope).

Cartoons
The following cinemas specialise in children's cartoons:
Cartoon Cinema Victoria Station, Buckingham Palace Road SW1.
Tel 834 7641
Oxford Street Cartoon Cinema Oxford Walk, 150 Oxford Street W1. Tel 834 6765

Children's Book Centre B6
229 Kensington High Street W8
Tube: High Street Kensington. Bus: 9, 27, 28, 33, 49, 73. Mon-Sat 9.30-6.
The largest children's bookshop in the country, helpfully divided into sections for different age groups. Toy shop upstairs.

Commonwealth Institute B6
Kensington High Street W8
Tube, bus and opening times p. 62
This excitingly designed, modern exhibition centre has permanent displays on all the Commonwealth countries, and studies on wildlife. Helpful guides, quiz sheets and films, plus a shop selling ethnic souvenirs.

Cutty Sark and Gypsy Moth IV GL D2
King William Walk,
Greenwich Pier SE10
British Rail: Greenwich. Boat from Tower, Charing Cross and Westminster Piers. Bus: 53, 54, 75, 177, 180, 185. Mon-Sat 11-6 (5 in winter), Sun 2.30-6 (5 in winter), Adm fee
The *Cutty Sark* is the last of those beautiful sailing ships, the 'tea-clippers', which raced round the Horn with their cargoes of tea. Its 3000 sq yds of rigging is now carefully labelled to show how they got it up and down. Also on view are the sailors' cabins, the gallery complete with old furnishings, and a collection of ships' figureheads. Alongside is the much smaller *Gypsy Moth IV*, in which Sir Francis Chichester sailed single-handed around the world in 1966.

Geffrye Museum N1
Kingsland Road E2
Tube, bus and opening times p. 62
This museum has a series of room-sets showing the decor and furniture of different periods from 1600 to the 1930s. There is a programme of special projects for schools during term time or for any child over 7 during the holidays or on Saturdays (sessions at 10am and 2pm).

Hamley's G4
188 Regent Street W1
Tube: Oxford Circus, Piccadilly, Bond Street. Bus: 3, 6, 12, 13, 15, 23, 53, 88, 500. Mon-Sat 9-5.30
The biggest toyshop in the world, with every conceivable toy and game. The 4th floor has a huge display area.

Hampton Court Palace
See *Historic Buildings* p. 49

Horniman Museum GL C3
100 London Road SE23
Tube, bus and opening times p. 64
This small and fascinating museum, specifically aimed at children, follows the theme of Man and His Environment, illustrating his beliefs and progress from prehistoric times. There are masks and shrunken heads, Eskimo art, an aquarium, musical instruments and a natural history section with animals and a working beehive.

Institute of Contemporary Arts H5
Children's Cinema Club
Nash House, The Mall SW1. Tel 930 3647
Tube, bus and opening times p. 65
Special programme of films for children on Saturday and Sunday afternoons at 3pm.

Kew Bridge Engines Museum GL B2
Green Dragon Lane, Brentford, Middlesex
British Rail: Kew Bridge. Tube: Gunnersbury then bus 237, 267. Bus: 15, 65. Sat & Sun only 11-5. Adm fee
Some of the biggest and oldest steam engines in the world in operation, plus a working display of pumping stations.

Lee Valley Park GL D1
Myddelton House, Bulls Cross, Enfield,
Middlesex. Tel Lee Valley 717711.
British Rail: Broxbourne. Bus: 735 Green Line
The Lee Valley Park covers some 23m from
Bow Road to Ware, Hertfordshire. It offers
many leisure, recreation and sports facilities,
including the Picketts Lock Sports Centre.
Of special interest are: Hayes Hill Farm – a
traditional farmyard with 16th c. barn; Lee
Valley Park Lido – an indoor bathing pool
with wave makers, underwater lighting and
simulated beach; the Waterbus from
Broxbourne Boatyard on Sunday afternoons
(also Wed, Thur and Fri during school
holidays) and rowing or motorboats.

Little Angel Marionette Theatre K1
14 Dagmar Passage, Cross Street N1.
Tel 226 1787
Tube: Angel, Highbury and Islington. Bus: 4, 19,
30, 38, 43, 73, 104, 171, 279. Adm fee
A world famous theatre, specifically built for
puppets, with performances on Saturday and
Sunday afternoons at 3pm as well as some
during the week and school holidays. Show
for the under 5's at 11am on Saturdays.
Bookings by phone.

London Butterfly House GL B2
Syon Park, Brentford, Middlesex
Tube: Gunnersbury then bus 237 or 267 to Syon
Park Gate. Bus: 37. Daily 10-5. Adm fee
Converted greenhouse with free-flying
butterflies in attractive setting of Syon Park.
(See *Parks, Gardens & Zoos* p. 75)

London Dungeon M5
34 Tooley Street SE1
Tube: London Bridge. Bus: 8A, 10, 21, 35, 40, 43,
44, 47, 48, 95, 133, 501, 513. Apr-Sep, daily 10-6,
Oct-Mar, daily 10-4. Adm fee
Life-size reconstructions of torture and
death exhibited in huge dark vaults. Not
suitable for children under 14.

London Planetarium F3
Marylebone Road NW1
Tube: Baker Street. Bus: 1, 2, 2B, 13, 30, 74, 113,
159. Daily 11-4.30. Adm fee
Like being out of doors on a clear night, with
an expert guide to explain and the Zeiss Star
projector to transport the viewer through
space and time. Also Laser light concerts in
the evening (Tel 486 2242 for details).

London Transport Museum J4
Covent Garden WC2
Tube, bus and opening times p. 65
Trolleybuses, trams and steam trains
illustrate the history of London Transport
since 1829. Children can climb aboard, work
the points and signals, operate the controls
of a tube train and drive a tram. Film shows
and other activities at weekends.

London Zoo F1
See *Parks, Gardens & Wildlife* p. 75

Madame Tussaud's F3
Marylebone Road NW1
Tube, bus and opening times p. 65
The oldest and largest waxworks exhibition
in the world with an ever-changing selection
of famous figures, including historical
characters, film stars, pop singers,
sportsmen and politicians. The Chamber of
Horrors has murderers, hangmen and
assassins and there is a Sleeping Beauty who
actually breathes.

National Film Theatre J5
South Bank SE1. Tel 928 3232
Tube: Waterloo. Bus: 1, 4, 68, 70, 76, 149, 168A,
171, 176, 188, 239, 501, 502, 503, 507, 513
Films for children on Saturday and Sunday
afternoons at 4pm.

National Theatre J5
Upper Ground SE1. Tel 928 2252
Tube and bus as National Film Theatre
Backstage tours of the three auditoriums and
workshops last 1¼ hours and run from
Mon-Sat at 10.15, 12.30 (not Wed & Sat),
12.45, 5.30 (not Wed & Sat), 6. Tickets from
the Lyttleton Information Desk.

Natural History Museum
See *Museums* p. 67

Palladium Cellars G4
8 Argyll Street W1. Tel 734 5776
Tube: Oxford Circus. Bus: 1, 6, 7, 8, 12, 13, 15,
16A, 23, 73, 88, 113, 159, 500. Mon-Sat 10-8, Sun
12-6. Adm fee
Right under the London Palladium, the
'Underworld of Entertainment' has over 100
lifesize figures, many moving and speaking,
presenting a variety of tableaux from
Elizabethan theatre to space flight.

Play Parks
There are play parks during the school
holidays from 11-6 at: Battersea Park,
Crystal Palace Park, Finsbury Park, Holland
Park and Parliament Hill Fields.

Polka Children's Theatre GL B3
240 The Broadway SW19. Tel 543 4888
British Rail: Wimbledon. Tube: Wimbledon, South
Wimbledon. Tue-Sat 10-4.30. Adm fee
Morning and afternoon performances plus
an exhibition of puppets and toys. There are
also children's workshops ranging from
puppet and toy making to mime and dance.
Birthday parties a speciality.

Pollock's Toy Museum H3
1 Scala Street W1
Tube: Goodge Street. Bus: 14, 24, 29, 73, 176.
Mon-Sat 10-5. Adm fee
A tiny museum crammed with antique toys
including the oldest teddy bear in England,
Victorian toy theatres, dolls' houses, peep
shows and magic lanterns. A good toyshop
offers a range of cut-out theatres, miniatures
and old-fashioned toys.

Science Museum D6
Exhibition Road SW7
Tube, bus and opening times p. 68

The history and application of science are demonstrated with working models, including mine pumps, early aeroplanes and the oldest locomotive in the world. The Children's Gallery, with its models and machines, provides endless opportunities for do-it-yourself wizardry.

Thorpe Park GL A3
Staines Lane, Chertsey, Surrey KT16 8PN. Tel 09328 62633
On A320 between Chertsey and Staines. (Green Line buses and Alder Valley buses stop at park). Easter fortnight, Jun-mid Sep daily, mid Sep-Oct weekends only, 10-6. Evenings (Fri-Sun 7.30-11) in summer season. Adm fee

Britain's first theme park, covering 450 acres of lakes and landscaped parkland. The central theme features the origins, history and achievements of the British people, with re-creations of a Celtic farmhouse, Roman fort, Viking longship, World War I airfield, etc. Scale models of more than 40 of the world's famous monuments, from the Pyramid of Cheops to the Space Shuttle. Water gardens, model farm, go-kart racing and children's amusements. Travel around in an open carriage decorated like an old-fashioned traction engine or a waterbus on the lake. Cinema 180 is the latest in realistic cinema technology: the viewer becomes part of the action. Special attractions daily.

Tower Bridge N5
SE1. Tel 407 0922
Tube: Tower Hill. Bus: 23, 42, 70, 78. Apr-Oct, daily 10-6.30, Nov-Mar 10-4.45. Adm fee

One of London's most famous landmarks, completed in 1894 and at one time opening for the passage of ships up to 50 times a day. The original hydraulic engines can be seen, with a film explaining how they work, and a special exhibition traces the history of London's bridges from Roman times. The enclosed walkway between the two towers offers a splendid view of the city.

Unicorn Theatre for Children H4
6 Great Newport Street WC2. Tel 836 3334
Tube: Leicester Square. Bus: 24, 29, 176. Adm fee

A variety of plays and children's shows, suitable for 4-12 year olds, with performances on weekend afternoons (2.30) and during the week for school groups.

Wembley Stadium GL B2
Wembley Park, Middlesex. Tel 902 8833
British Rail: Wembley Complex. Tube: Wembley Park. Bus: 18, 83, 92, 182, 297. Tours of the stadium daily (not Thur) 10-12, 2-4. Adm fee
Conducted tours on the hour behind the scenes. Visits to the changing rooms along the same passage the players use and up the 39 steps to where the cups are received.

Ceremonies & Events

DAILY

Ceremony of the Keys
Tower of London EC3
9.40pm
Said to be the world's oldest military ceremony. Each night the Chief Warder, dressed in Beefeater costume and accompanied by an escort of the Brigade of Guards, locks up the main towers and West Gate. *Attendance by prior application to the Governor.*

Changing of the Guard
Buckingham Palace SW1
11.30am (alternate days in winter)
Traditional parade with much pomp and ceremony, when the Guard changes in front of the Palace. Very crowded in summer, though even then a good view of the Guards marching to and from the Palace (from Chelsea or Wellington Barracks) can be had en route. *Phone London Tourist Board for details.*

Changing of the Horse Guards
Horse Guards Arch, Whitehall W1
Mon-Sat 11am, Sun 10am
With their shining armour and plumed helmets, the Queen's mounted Guards leave Hyde Park Barracks at 10.30am and proceed down the Mall for parade at Horse Guards in Whitehall, where the Changing of the Guard ceremony takes place inside the forecourt.

Speaker's Procession
Houses of Parliament SW1
Mon-Fri 2.25pm (when Parliament is sitting)
The Speaker in ceremonial attire proceeds through the lobby to open the day's debate in the House of Commons. The policemen on duty raise their helmets in unique traditional salute. *Apply to police officer on duty.*

ANNUAL

January

International Boat Show
Earls Court, Warwick Road SW5
Early Jan
Europe's largest Boat Show, with exhibits displaying the latest yachts, motor launches and nautical equipment.

Epiphany Gifts
Chapel Royal, St James's Palace, Marlborough Road SW1
Jan 6
The service begins at 11.30 and is attended by the Queen. Three purses, symbolizing gold, frankincense and myrrh are presented by two gentlemen ushers, and later distributed to the poor of the parish.

Chinese New Year
Gerrard Street, Soho W1
Jan-Mar Sun
Annual celebration for the Chinese community, with a colourful procession of huge paper dragons and lanterns to mark the start of the Year. *Ask in local shops for exact date.*

Anniversary of King Charles I's Execution
Trafalgar Square WC2
Jan 30
Ceremony held, with laying of wreaths, beneath Charles I statue in Trafalgar Square.

February

Anniversary of Queen Elizabeth II's Accession
Hyde Park W1
Feb 6
41-gun salute at 12 noon by the King's Troop of the Royal Horse Artillery, and at 1pm at Tower of London by the Honourable Artillery Company. Salutes are also fired on the Queen's birthday (April 21), Prince Philip's birthday (June 2), Queen's Official Birthday (2nd Sat in June), and Queen Mother's birthday (Aug 4).

Crufts Dog Show
Earls Court, Warwick Road SW5
Early Feb
Over 8000 dogs of many different breeds competing for 'Champion of the Year' awards.

March

Ideal Home Exhibition
Earls Court, Warwick Road SW5
Mid Mar
London's most popular annual show, with exhibits of all that's new in interior design.

Oxford and Cambridge Boat Race
River Thames, Putney to Mortlake
Mar-Apr Sat
Celebrated university boat race, in which the two 'eights' battle it out over the traditional 4-mile course. Try watching from one of the riverside pubs by Hammersmith Bridge. Race starts according to the tide.

Spring Antiques Fair
Chelsea Old Town Hall, King's Road SW3
Mid Mar
London's premier antiques fair: all kinds of bric-a-brac and rarities.

April

Easter Fair
Hampstead Heath NW3
Easter Sun-Mon
All the fun of the biggest fair in England, with every conceivable stall and ride spread out over three sites on the Heath.

Easter Parade
Battersea Park SW11
Easter Sun
Picturesque carnival procession of ladies wearing Easter bonnets ranging from the spectacular to the ludicrous, preceded by a parade of old and vintage vehicles.

May

Chelsea Flower Show
Royal Hospital Grounds, Chelsea SW3
Late May
Spectacular annual display of horticultural art, with many rare and exotic blooms.

Oak Apple Day
Royal Hospital, Chelsea SW3
May 29
Inspection of the 'Chelsea Pensioners' in their red topcoats. Ceremony celebrates the escape (by hiding in an oak tree) of the hospital's founder, Charles II.

Royal Academy Exhibition
Burlington House, Piccadilly W1
Jul/Aug
A regular event since 1769, the Royal Academy's Summer Exhibition contains paintings, sculptures and designs by living artists from all over the country. Wide variety of largely mainstream art.

June

Trooping the Colour
Horse Guards Parade, Whitehall W1
Sat nearest Jun 11
London's most spectacular military parade. The celebration of the Queen's Official Birthday is marked by a parade of the Brigade of Guards. This 2-hour pageant has its origins in the 16th c., when the colours were paraded before each man in the regiment. The intricate march-past includes the massed bands of five regiments, and is acknowledged by the Queen on horseback. Apply between Jan-Mar to HQ Household Division, Horse Guards, London SW1

All England Lawn Tennis Championships
Wimbledon SW19
Last week Jun-1st week Jul
Wimbledon Fortnight, when the stars of world tennis play for the premier title. Apply for Centre and No 1 Courts, tickets from Oct 1 onwards, or queue for standing room on the day. Tel 946 2244 for details.

July

Doggett's Coat and Badge Race
London Bridge to Chelsea
Late Jul
Oldest boat race in the world – traditional single sculls race for Thames Watermen dating from 1716. Winner receives a scarlet coat and badge, first presented by the actor Thomas Doggett.

Promenade Concerts

Royal Albert Hall, Kensington Gore SW7
Late Jul-Sep

A season of concerts founded by Sir Henry
Wood in 1895 with the idea of bringing
classical music within popular range. Low
price 'Promenade' tickets for areas without
seats obtained by queuing on the night. *Box
Office: Tel 589 8212*

Royal International Horse Show

Empire Pool, Wembley, Middlesex
Mid Jul

Stars of the show-jumping world compete
for premier trophies. Phone 235 5390 for
tickets and details.

Royal Tournament

Earls Court, Warwick Road SW5
2 weeks mid Jul

Spectacular show with feats of military
expertise and daring, marching and brass
bands. Phone 930 6000 for details.

August

Notting Hill Carnival

Notting Hill W11

London's answer to the Rio Carnival, with
floats of steel bands followed by revellers and
dancers. An informal community event
which has evolved into London's greatest
street festival.

September

Autumn Antiques Fair

Chelsea Old Town Hall, Kings Road SW3
Mid Sep
See *Spring Fair*, March

Battle of Britain Day

Over central London
Sep 15

RAF fly-past between 11-12, sometimes
featuring the famous Red Devils Squadron
in formation flying – to commemorate the
defeat of Hitler's Luftwaffe in 1940.

October

Costermongers' Harvest Festival

St Martin-in-the-Fields, Trafalgar Square
WC2

1st Sun in Oct

London's own Harvest Festival, attended by
the famous Cockney 'Pearly Kings and
Queens' all dressed in their traditional
sequined regalia. Each monarch brings fruit,
flowers and vegetables and afterwards they
hold an informal get-together.

Opening of the Law Courts

Westminster Abbey SW1
Oct 1

Judges in their ceremonial wigs and robes
attend the Abbey service. Afterwards the
Lord Chancellor leads a procession across
Parliament Square to the House of Lords.

Trafalgar Day

Trafalgar Square WC2
Oct 21

Service and parade through the square, run
by the Navy League, to mark Lord Nelson's
victory over the French at Trafalgar in 1805.

November

Bonfire Night

Nov 5

Traditional burning of the 'Guy' – to mark
the discovery of Guy Fawkes' Gunpowder
Plot to blow up Parliament in 1605. Bonfires
and firework parties everywhere: suggest
Colville Square W11 and Primrose Hill.

London to Brighton Veteran Car Race

Starts Hyde Park Corner W1
1st Sun in Nov

Veteran cars set off for the 60-mile drive to
Brighton, with drivers and passengers in
period costumes.

Lord Mayor's Show

Guildhall to Law Courts, City
2nd Sat in Nov

Each year the aldermen of the city elect a
new Lord Mayor, and his year of office
begins with a spectacular procession through
the City. Marching bands and decorated
floats precede the new Lord Mayor in his
gilded state coach, guarded by pikemen.

Remembrance Day

Cenotaph, Whitehall SW1
2nd Sun in Nov

Service and wreath-laying ceremony to
commemorate the dead of both World Wars.
Attended by leading politicians and Royalty.
Two minutes' silence at 11am, followed by a
salute of guns and march-past.

State Opening of Parliament

Houses of Parliament SW1
Early Nov

The Queen in the Irish State Coach drives
from Buckingham Palace to Victoria Tower,
to speak to the members of both Houses. A
royal salute is fired in St James's Park.

December

Christmas Decorations

West End
Late Nov-early Dec

Elaborate illuminations decorate Regent and
Oxford Street. In Trafalgar Square the large
illuminated Christmas tree, donated each
year by the people of Norway, is switched
on. Special Westminster Carol Service is
held below the tree at a later date.

New Year's Eve Celebrations

Trafalgar Square WC2

High jinks and jollity to mark the year's end.
Thousands of people in festive mood take
over the square, with many 'cooling off' in
the freezing waters of the fountains.

Sport & Recreation

London and the surrounding area has a large number of sports centres with a wide range of different activities. Detailed information of what to do and where from the *London & SE Region Sports Council*, 160 Portland Street W1 (Tel 580 9092) or from the *Sports Council Information Centre*, 70 Brompton Road SW3 (Tel 589 3411). For tickets for sporting events contact *Keith Prowse Agencies* (Head Office Tel 637 3131) or the box office of the venue stadium.

Sports Centres with facilities for recreation and sport

Crystal Palace National Sports Centre
Ledrington Road, Crystal Palace SE19
Tel 778 0131
The largest multi-sports centre in the country, with facilities for 50 sports and a floodlit stadium that can hold 16,000 spectators. Olympic swimming and diving pools, dry-ski slope, indoor sports hall. Courses in many sports including skiing, squash and swimming. Yearly fee, plus a small amount for equipment and teaching. National and international events held here.

Lee Valley Regional Park
Myddleton House, Bulls Cross, Enfield.
Tel Lea Valley 717711
The only development of its kind in the UK, stretching for some 23m from Bow Road to Ware, Hertfordshire, using derelict ground for a range of leisure activities, including sailing, swimming and horse riding. (See also *Picketts Lock Sports Centre* below)

Michael Sobell Sports Centre
Hornsey Road N7. Tel 607 1632
Indoor centre with most sports: classes in archery, badminton, basketball, boxing, cricket, gymnastics, hockey, martial arts, netball, squash, table tennis, volleyball, weightlifting and yoga. Ice-rink, ski slope and sauna. Yearly and entrance fee.

Picketts Lock Sports Centre
Picketts Lock Lane N9. Tel 803 4756
This sports centre in the Lee Valley Regional Park offers a range of activities including: indoor soccer, gymnastics, badminton, basketball, hockey, netball, volleyball, martial arts, roller skating, shooting, bowls and swimming. Outdoor sports include: football, hockey, tennis and golf. Tuition available. Membership not necessary.

Swiss Cottage Sports Centre
Winchester Road NW3. Tel 278 4444
Several swimming pools, indoor badminton, basketball, gymnastics, martial arts, squash.

Thorpe Park
Staines Lane, Chertsey, Surrey KT16 8PN
Tel (09328) 62633
Britain's first theme park with 450 acres of lakes and landscaped parkland. An 'adventure in leisure' with its own waterski and board sailing schools, jetboats, rowing boats, bumper boats and pedaloes. Plus go-karting, crazy golf and triskating.

Wembley Complex
Wembley, Middlesex. Tel 902 8833
Wembley Stadium holds 100,000 under cover. International Squash Centre. Many international events held here including the FA Cup Final, ice shows, Rugby League Final, hockey, boxing, ice hockey, skating, tennis, basketball, netball, cycle races, greyhound racing, speedway and ice shows. Squash courts available. To book Tel 902 9230.

White City Pool
Bloemfontein Road W12. Tel 743 5544
Three pools, sauna, solarium and aerotone.

YMCA London Central
112 Great Russell Street WC1. Tel 637 8131
Indoor only. Badminton, basketball, gymnastics, martial arts, soccer, sub aqua, swimming, table tennis, volleyball and yoga. Membership fee.

Elephant and Castle Recreation Centre
22 Elephant and Castle SE1. Tel 582 5505
Squash, badminton, swimming, sauna, solarium, table tennis, volleyball, keep fit, basketball, five-a-side football.

Recreation

Boating
A large number of London's parks hire out boats; sailing in Hyde Park, Regent's Park and on the River Thames upriver from Putney. Payment by the hour.

Horse Riding
Riding in: Hyde Park, Hampstead Heath, Richmond Park, Wimbledon Common, Epping Forest, Hainault Forest and Dulwich Common.

Ice Skating
Main rinks are:
Queen's Ice Skating Club, 17 Queensway W2
Richmond Ice Rink, Clevedon Road, Twickenham, Middlesex
Silver Blades Ice Rink, 386 Streatham High Street SW16
Michael Sobell Sports Centre, Hornsey Road N7
All have an admission charge and will hire skates

Roller Skating
Alexandra Palace Roller Rink, Muswell Hill N22

Electric Ballroom Roller-disco, 184 Camden High Street NW1

Ten Pin Bowling
British Ten Pin Bowling Association, 19 Canterbury Avenue, Ilford, Essex, Tel 554 9173, will give information and advice.

Shopping & Markets

London ranks as one of the finest cities in the world for shopping. It caters for everything the visitor might wish to buy, and has retained a healthy balance of small, traditional shops and large department stores. For those with time, a browse around some of London's street markets is well worthwhile: the discerning buyer will find many a bargain waiting to be snapped up.

In general, shops in London are open from Monday to Saturday 9.30-5.30 (including lunchtime). Although London is not a late-night city, most shops in the West End stay open until at least 7pm on Thursdays (Wednesdays in Knightsbridge). On Sundays, with the exception of certain very cosmopolitan areas (Earls Court, for instance), all shops are closed (except newsagents which open in the morning). Sunday, on the other hand, is often the best day for markets.

Best buys in London are goods made in Great Britain, especially fabrics – hand-printed cottons, tweeds, tartans, cashmeres – and knitwear (Shetland, Guernsey, Fair Isle, etc.). Also, ready-to-wear clothes, both for adults and children. Other good buys are china and porcelain, in particular Wedgwood and Coleport, silver and antiques. Traditional English fare such as teas and cheese (Stilton, Cheddar etc.) represents good value for money. Major department stores and shops frequently dealing with overseas buyers are able to advise about arranging to have visitors' purchases sent abroad, free of Value Added Tax (VAT).

London's Great Stores

The most popular area for shopping is **Oxford Street**, in the heart of the West End, which brims over with shops selling casual clothes and shoes, and is the home of several major department stores, such as *Selfridges* and *John Lewis*. Nearby in Regent Street is *Liberty's*, famous for its fine silk and cotton dress and furnishing fabrics. *Knightsbridge* is another popular shopping centre and the home of *Harrods*, London's most exclusive store, which claims to be able to supply everything from a birthday cake to a grand piano. The area also includes *Harvey Nichols*, a select department store renowned for its *haute couture* clothes and accessories. 2m further W in **Kensington High Street** is *Barkers*, a good general-purpose store with departments on four floors. Two excellent household stores in **Tottenham Court Road** are *Heal's* and *Habitat*, which stock well-designed contemporary furnishings. To assist the potential buyer in his search for the right product, a *résumé* is given below of specific areas and shops where particular specialities can be found.

Antiques

London is possibly the best city in the world for antiques. *Asprey* in New Bond Street W1 is famous for rare and beautiful items. For antique furniture, especially 18th- and 19th-c., *Mallett* in the same street is highly recommended. Certain shops in nearby Mount Street W1 also specialise in Oriental as well as English pieces. For pewter and brass *Casimir* in Pembridge Road W11 is good. Ceramics are to be found at *Jellinek and Sampson*, Brompton Road SW3, while some beautiful porcelain may be bought at *Jean Sewell*, Campden Street W8. *Strike One* in Camden Passage N1 specialises in antique clocks of every kind. As well as the specialist shops, there are a number of indoor antique markets, stocking a wide selection of antiques, such as that in *Barrett Street* W1 and the *Kensington Hypermarket*, in Kensington High Street. *Grays* in Davies Mews W1 is the largest of this type of market. *King's Road* SW3 is a good area containing both *Antiquarius* and *Chenil's*. There are also various street markets which specialise in antiques (see below). *Camden Passage*, Islington N1 combines both covered shops and outside stalls.

Art Dealers

Most are centred in Mayfair and St. James's. For old masters *Agnew's* and *Colnaghi* are recommended, both in Old Bond Street W1, while *The Fine Art Society*, New Bond Street W1 deals in English watercolours. For sporting prints, *Ackerman* also in Old Bond Street is hard to beat, while the *Parke Gallery* in Albermarle Street W1 has a fine collection of seascapes. Dutch and Flemish paintings of the Renaissance period can be found at *L. Koester*, Duke Street SW1. Contemporary art dealers include *Brook Street Gallery*, Brook Street W1.

Books

Charing Cross Road is an excellent area for books in general, with *Foyles*, the largest bookshop in London, *Collet's*, and numerous second-hand booksellers. *Dillons* in Malet Street WC1 is good for academic books, while *Hatchards* in Piccadilly is London's oldest bookshop and has a good general cross-section. For books on and in foreign languages, best is *Grant & Cutler*, tucked away in Buckingham Street WC2. Antiquarian books can be found at *Quaritch*, Lower John Street W1. For children's books, the *Children's Book Centre*, Kensington High Street W8; for maps and guides *Stanfords* of Long Acre WC2.

China and Glass

Besides the department stores, which stock general china and glass, the more specialist shops are to be found in Regent Street W1. *Lawleys* and *Rosenthal* sell their own china, while *Gered* deals in Wedgwood. *Habitat*,

Tottenham Court Road W1 and King's Road SW3 are excellent for modern designs, and the *China Reject Shop* in Beauchamp Place SW3 sells seconds. China and crystal can be found at *Thomas Goode*, South Audley Street W1, while old glass can be obtained from *Howard Phillips*, Henrietta Place W1.

Clothing & Knitwear

For women, the most exclusive boutiques are to be found in Knightsbridge (Beauchamp Place, Brompton Road, Sloane Street in particular), but also in the West End – Regent Street, New Bond Street, South Molton Street and St Christopher's Place. Kensington High Street and Oxford Street are for more casual clothes, while King's Road is for high-fashion. Jermyn Street and Bond Street (both Old and New) are excellent for men's clothes. Also in the West End, Regent Street, Piccadilly, Savile Row and St James's Street are recommended. For children, *Marks & Spencer* and *Mothercare* in Oxford Street are excellent. *Hennes* in Kensington High Street is also good. *Rowes*, New Bond Street, W1 is where the royal children are clad. For knitwear, *Marks & Spencer* is unbeatable for simple styles, while the more ornate can be found at *The Scotch House* (in the West End and Knightsbridge), *Scottish Merchant*, Covent Garden WC2 and *Westaway & Westaway*, Great Russell Street WC1. The latter sells the cheapest quality knitwear in London.

Food

Fortnum & Mason, Piccadilly W1, *Harrods* Food Hall and *Selfridges* excel in exotic and unusual food. Health foods are available at *Ceres Bakery* in Portobello Road W11 and *Cranks* in Marshall Street W1. For cheeses of every kind *Paxton and Whitfield* in Jermyn Street SW1 are excellent, while *Justin de Blank* in Elizabeth Street SW1 specialises in French cheeses. Soho contains numerous delicatessens and foodshops with continental specialities.

Jewellery

Hatton Garden is the centre of the precious stone trade in London. There are also excellent jewellers elsewhere, such as *Asprey*, New Bond Street W1. *Cartier*, in the same street, sells exclusive jewellery. For antique jewellery *Andrew Grima*, Jermyn Street SW1 and *S. J. Phillips* New Bond Street W1 are specialists. *Garrard's* in Regent Street W1 is also very select and responsible for the upkeep of the Crown Jewels.

Silver

Dealers in antique and modern silver are to be found in the *London Silver Vaults*, Chancery Lane WC2. *Asprey* and *The Silver Galleries* in New Bond Street W1 are also good. *Hatton Garden* houses some silver dealers.

Toys

Hamleys in Regent Street, W1 is the toy-lover's mecca. There is also *Pollock's Toy Museum*, Scala Street W1 for historical and traditional toys. *James Galt*, Great Marlborough Street W1 is excellent for educational, wooden toys.

Street Markets

Selling everything from Peruvian pullovers to Cornish cabbage, street markets are a traditional part of London life, guaranteed to entertain, if not always to provide what you are looking for. They are full of colourful, quick-witted characters, often Cockney in origin, who vocally promote their wares above the hustle and bustle of the market. Watch out for 'sharks' though – traders who have been known to conjure up mouldy apples from under the counter or bounce a purchase off the scales before the customer has a chance to check the weight.

RETAIL MARKETS

Berwick Street
Soho W1
Mon-Sat 9-5
Lively general market with the emphasis on fruit and vegetables.

Camden Lock
Camden High Street NW1
Sat & Sun 10-5.30
Young, ethnic market specialising in crafts, made on the premises, such as stained glass, pottery, sandals and jewellery. Also clothes, hand-knitted jumpers, antiques and bric-a-brac.

Camden Passage
Off Upper Street, Islington N1
Tue, Wed & Sat 8-4; Thur & Fri 9-5
Attractive antique centre with a variety of small shops and open-air stalls selling general antiques and bric-a-brac. On Thursday and Friday the market specialises in books, prints and drawings.

Chapel Street
White Conduit Street N1
Daily 8-5
Mainly a fruit and vegetable market, but with bric-a-brac and second-hand clothes at weekends. Busiest on Sundays.

Church Street
Marylebone W2
Mon-Sat 9-6
Lively, general market with a variety of antiques and second-hand furniture. Best days, Friday and Saturday.

Farringdon Road
EC1
Mon-Fri 12-2, Sat 10-12
A handful of stalls selling old books, manuscripts, paperbacks, prints and music. This market is frequented by dealers and is relatively unknown to the general public.

Greenwich Antiques Market
High Road SE10
Sat 8-4 & Sun in summer
A selection of antiques within a short
distance of the *Cutty Sark*.

Jubilee Market
Southampton Street WC2
Mon-Sat 9-4.30
Small market which varies its specialities
according to the day of the week: on Monday
it is antiques, Tuesday to Friday general,
and on weekends it specialises in crafts
(pottery, knitwear, glass and jewellery etc.).

Leadenhall Market
Gracechurch Street EC3
Mon-Fri 9-5
Beautiful Victorian covered market in the
heart of the City, specialising in poultry and
game, general provisions and plants. The
arcade also contains a number of pubs.

Leather Lane
EC1
Mon-Fri 10-2
Once a leather mart,now mainly fruit and
vegetables, clothes, shoes, fabrics and
bric-a-brac.

New Caledonian Market
Bermondsey Square, Tower Bridge Road
SE1
Fri 5am-2pm
This is where the dealers buy antiques. The
early bird gets the better bargain!

Petticoat Lane
Middlesex Street E1
Sun 9-2
Famous Sunday market offering wares of
every kind at prices which undercut the
shops. Always crowded and noisy: the
atmosphere is unique.

Portobello Road
Off Westbourne Park W11
Sat 9-5
Lively market selling bric-a-brac, antiques,
old clothes and jewellery.

WHOLESALE MARKETS

As well as the retail street markets, there are
a number of wholesale markets where
members of the public are tolerated so long
as they do not impede business. These are
open in the early morning.

Borough Market
Southwark SE1
Mon-Sat 3.30-7am
Claimed to be the oldest municipal fruit and
vegetable market in London.

Smithfield
Charterhouse Street EC1
Mon-Thur 5-12, Fri 5-7am
This famous meat market stands on a site
used as a cattle market in the 14th-c. It is
vast and an impressive sight with its rows of
carcasses.

Spitalfields
Commercial Street E1
Mon-Sat 4.30-10am
This fruit, vegetable and flower market was
founded in 1682. It is now split into two
halls, with fruit and vegetables in one and
flowers in the other.

CRAFTS

The British Crafts Council, 12 Waterloo Place
SW1 will supply general information on craft
shops, galleries, exhibitions, suppliers of
material and equipment, museums featuring
crafts and crafts publications. Work by
carefully selected craftsmen may be
commissioned from the Council. Below is a
list of some craft shops and their specialities.

Argenta Gallery
82 Fulham Road SW3
A collection of contemporary jewellery, all
by independent jewellers in the UK.

Aspects
3-5 Whitfield Street W1
New gallery specialising in modern
experimental jewellery. Changing
exhibitions of work in other media.

British Crafts Centre
43 Earlham Street WC2
Exhibits and sells selected work in a variety
of crafts.

Craft Shop V & A
Victoria & Albert Museum, South
Kensington SW7
Sells modern crafts, from ceramics and glass
to textiles and jewellery.

Craftsmen Potters' Shop
William Blake House, Marshall Street W1
Decorative and functional pottery by
members of the Craftsmen Potters'
Association.

Electrum
21 South Molton Street W1
Contemporary jewellers display and sell their
work.

The Glasshouse
65 Long Acre WC2
Glassblowers on the premises exhibit and sell
work, from plates to goblets.

The Irish Shop
11 Duke Street W1
Waterford crystal and Belleek china, along
with knitwear, clothes and general Irish
crafts.

The Scotch House
2 Brompton Road, Knightsbridge SW1 (and
branches)
Excellent selection of Scottish woollens,
including tartans.

London's Waterways

The Thames The city of London grew up along the banks of the River Thames, which winds its way east 210 miles from the Cotswolds to the North Sea. Along the 42-mile stretch that belongs to London, you can see much of the vivid history of England's capital. The river, however, never recovered from the wartime destruction and in post-war years the 'Pool of London' became obsolete as the city's port. With the major shift of cargo transport to the roads, and the extension of the modern container port to the east at Tilbury, few large ships now venture further up-river. Many of the docks are closed and the future of those that remain is uncertain, with most of London's dockland scheduled for redevelopment.

But if the Thames is no longer filled with barges, tugs and ocean-going liners, it is still very much at the centre of London life. Many annual events take place on its waters – the Oxford and Cambridge boat race, the Doggett's Coat and Badge Race and the medieval custom of Swan Upping, or the counting and marking of swans.

A Trip on the Thames

Many of London's historic landmarks line the banks of its river and it's now possible to walk along a footpath for the entire stretch from Putney Bridge upstream to Hampton Court. From Putney downstream to Tower Bridge there are many embankments and riverside parks, so that the N or S bank is usually accessible.

But one of the best ways to see the river is by boat. During the summer months riverboats sail from the piers at Westminster, Charing Cross and the Tower of London upstream to Kew, Richmond and Hampton Court, and downstream to Greenwich.

Following the river from the beautiful 16th-c. palace of Hampton Court, the Thames winds past the green acres of Hampton Court Park and on below Kingston Bridge to Teddington Lock, which marks the end of the tideway.

The river flows on N past Twickenham, where Marble Hill House and park face Ham House on the opposite side. On to Richmond, with its Old Deer Park where the deer still roam: a superb view of the Thames Valley can be had from Richmond Hill.

Continuing on to Chiswick, the river passes between the green banks of Kew Gardens and Syon Park, then changes to an urban aspect as it enters W London. Crossed by frequent bridges, the river is now confined by stone embankments which mark the start of the heart of London.

Of the many bridges that cross the river, perhaps Westminster, London and Tower Bridges have the most interesting history. Until 1750, London Bridge, rebuilt many times, was the only crossing over the river, and along the bridge itself were shops and houses. But in that year a new bridge was constructed in stone at Westminster (rebuilt in 1862). Following this the buildings on London Bridge were knocked down and the entire structure was replaced in 1832. This in turn was sold to the USA (to be re-erected in Arizona!) and replaced by the present modern span in 1972.

Tower Bridge, the last across the Thames, with its familiar Gothic towers, was completed in 1894, but nowadays it is rarely called upon to open its twin bascules to allow ships to pass through to the Pool of London (the highest point on the river that can be reached by large sea-going vessels). However, its magnificent lattice-work footbridge, closed in 1910, has recently been glassed in and is now once again open to the public.

Just upstream of Tower Bridge, facing the Tower of London, *HMS Belfast* is permanently moored as a floating naval museum. This 11,500-ton ship is the last survivor of the Royal Navy's Second World War cruisers.

On the N bank, adjacent to the Tower of London, is St Katharine's Dock. This has been successfully redeveloped as a yacht haven, and some of the early 19th-c. warehouses have been carefully restored. The dock itself houses an exhibition of historic ships, among them the famous *Discovery* in which Captain Scott made his first expedition to the Antarctic.

Downstream from Tower Bridge, the Thames passes through a landscape of sadly declining dockland interspersed with new developments. This was once the world's greatest port, with docks stretching from here as far E as Woolwich. At the next bend, between Wapping and Rotherhithe, the river passes over the first tunnel to be built beneath it. This is the old Thames Tunnel (completed 1843) which now carries the Whitechapel-New Cross Underground Line. The Blackwall and other tunnels were built later.

As the river loops around the Isle of Dogs there is the first glimpse of the tall rigging of the tea clipper, the *Cutty Sark*, which signals arrival at Greenwich. Here is the home of the Royal Naval College, Old Royal Observatory and the National Maritime Museum, which is centred on the magnificent Queen's House built by Inigo Jones (see *Museums* p. 67).

Further downstream still, at Woolwich Reach, the massive Thames Barrier is the world's largest movable flood barrier and is designed to stop surge tides flooding a large area of London.

The Canals With the Industrial Revolution came the canals, built to transport goods and raw materials from the industrial Midlands to the ports. The Grand Junction Canal (now part of the Grand Union) was London's first link with the Midlands, and canal boats carrying vital cargo travelled from Brentford in Middlesex to Braunston in Northamptonshire. The Paddington arm of this canal, from Bull's Bridge, Southall, to Paddington was opened in 1801; and the Regent's Canal, from Paddington to the Thames at Limehouse, was completed in 1820.

Unfortunately the canals were no match for the railways and by the 1850s the steam trains were carrying most of the freight to the docks. Today the capital's living canals are part of the Grand Union Canal (amalgamated in 1929) and the River Lea Navigation, which comes from Hertford into NE London, joining the Thames at Canning Town.

Until recently the Grand Union carried some cargo, but now only the River Lea Navigation is still used as a commercial waterway. But stripped of their commercial role, the canals are adapting to a new one. The towpaths are being opened up as walks and pleasure boats make use of the waterways.

The Regent's Canal

One of London's most attractive waterways, with a well-kept towpath between Lisson Grove and City Road. 8½ m long, the canal has two tunnels – Maida Hill and Islington. The locks at Camden Town start the drop down to the Thames at Limehouse, where Regent's Canal Dock lies silent and empty, destined for redevelopment.

The canal begins at Little Venice, near Paddington, a pretty basin where many decorative canal boats are moored. From Warwick Avenue Bridge, a few yards away, the first stretch of the canal flows between an avenue of fine houses, leading to Maida Hill Tunnel. There is no towpath here and it is necessary to go overground to Lisson Grove, the first of many access points.

From Lisson Grove there is an uninterrupted towpath walk through Regent's Park, where the Zoo flanks both sides of the canal and there is a free view of antelopes, camels and Lord Snowdon's unique aviary. Past the Zoo, the canal turns sharply left to Camden Lock, now a craft centre with a restaurant and even a dance hall. An hour or two can be spent exploring the thriving market which is held here.

Beyond Camden Lock, the canal is hemmed in by old and new buildings with little greenery to relieve the eye. At St Pancras Lock, the canal opens out into what is now a yacht basin with a backdrop view of the neo-Gothic spires of St Pancras Station. A little further on the canal widens out and Battlebridge Basin comes into sight lined with disused wharves.

Past Caledonian Road, Islington Tunnel ends this section of the towpath and it is necessary to go overground again to pick up the canal at the top of Noel Road. Here, the canal changes again with elegant houses and gardens lining its route. The Regent's Canal walk ends at City Road Lock and Basin, where sailing boats have taken the place of canal boats and skyscrapers dot the skyline.

River trips

During the summer these trips are available:

Downstream

Westminster Pier – Tower (20 min)
Westminster Pier – Greenwich (45 min)
Charing Cross Pier – Tower (20 min)
Charing Cross Pier – Greenwich (45 min)
Tower Pier – Greenwich (35 min)

Upstream

Tower Pier – Westminster (20 min)
Westminster Pier – Kew (1½ hrs)
Westminster Pier – Richmond (2½ hrs)
Westminster Pier – Hampton Court (3-5 hrs)

For details of sailings, fares and winter services phone 930 2062 (summer) or London Tourist Board's Riverboat Information Service on 839 2349.

Riverside pubs and restaurants

There are many fascinating and historic pubs along the river, from *The City Barge* at Chiswick to *The Prospect of Whitby* in Wapping. For details of these and other pubs and restaurants that overlook the river, phone the London Tourist Board: 730 0791 from 9-5.30 (Mon-Fri).

Canal trips

Jason's Trip

Opp. 60 Blomfield Road W9
Tel 286 3428. Tube: Warwick Avenue
Apr-Oct. Boat departs from Blomfield Road (Little Venice) daily for one-way or round trips to Camden Lock at 2 & 4pm (plus 11am from June).

Jenny Wren

250 Camden High Street NW1
Tel 485 4433/6210. Tube: Camden Town
Mar-Oct. Boat departs from Camden Lock daily for round trip to Little Venice at 2 & 3.30pm.

Zoo Waterbus

Delamere Terrace W2
Tel 286 6101. Tube: Warwick Avenue
Apr-Sep. Boat departs from Little Venice daily for trip to the Zoo on the hour 10-5.15pm (10-6.15pm Sun & Bank Hol). Service slightly less frequent Apr-May & Sep. Boat also departs from Zoo Waterbus landing-stage for one-way and round trip to Little Venice. Entrance to the Zoo optional.

Hotels (Trusthouse Forte)

Barkston Hotel
Barkston Gardens SW5
Tel 373 7851
Pleasantly situated overlooking a garden square next to Earl's Court Road close to the Exhibition Centre.

Brown's Hotel
Albermarle & Dover Street W1
Tel 493 6020
From 1837-59 James Brown, Lord Byron's butler, ran an elegant house here as a hotel for nobility and gentry – his ideals of service are faithfully maintained. The *L'Aperitif Restaurant* has a world-wide reputation.

Cavendish Hotel
Jermyn Street SW1
Tel 930 2111
Near Piccadilly, this modern hotel was built on the site of Rosa Lewis's *Cavendish Hotel*. The public rooms contain reminders of the Edwardian era in which she lived and the *Ribblesdale Restaurant* is named after her great friend, Lord Ribblesdale.

Cumberland Hotel
Marble Arch W1
Tel 262 1234
One of London's biggest hotels, overlooking Hyde Park and within easy distance of many major attractions. The *Wyvern Restaurant* specialises in English food.

Grosvenor House
Park Lane W1
Tel 499 6363
One of the truly great hotels of London and a favourite with many distinguished guests. Built by Sir Edwin Lutyens and called a 'city of hospitality'. Facilities include serviced apartments, shops, bars and restaurants, including the famous *90 Park Lane*.

Hyde Park Hotel
Knightsbridge SW1
Tel 235 2000
Overlooking Hyde Park, this international hotel is famous for its cuisine (the *Hyde Park Grill* is renowned) and high standard of personal service. Built in the Edwardian era it has lost none of its style or elegance.

Kensington Close Hotel
Wrights Lane W8
Tel 937 8170
In a quiet lane just off Kensington High Street this hotel is well-situated for holiday and business travel.

Post House Hotel
Haverstock Hill NW3
Tel 794 8121
Located near Hampstead village and the Heath, this modern 140-bedroom hotel has 50 family rooms and a free car park.

Regent Palace Hotel
Piccadilly Circus W1
Tel 734 7000
Set in the heart of the West End, this world-famous hotel is one of the largest in Europe with more than 1000 rooms, bars, shops and restaurants.

Hotel Russell
Russell Square WC1
Tel 837 6470
Overlooking one of London's finest squares, this hotel was opened on Derby Day 1900. Its marbled foyer is very fine and there are many magnificent rooms.

St George's Hotel
Langham Place W1
Tel 580 0111
Occupying the top six floors of the 14-storey Henry Wood House, the hotel has panoramic views over the city. It stands on the site of the old Queen's Hall (bombed in the war), where the Promenade Concerts were first held.

Strand Palace Hotel
Strand WC2
Tel 836 8080
Conveniently placed between the City and West End, this hotel has an international reputation and is popular with visitors.

Waldorf Hotel
Aldwych WC2
Tel 836 2400
Opened in 1908, this hotel is situated in the heart of London's theatreland. Its splendid Palm Court Lounge has retained all the elegance of the Edwardian era.

Westbury Hotel
New Bond Street W1
Tel 629 7755
A luxury hotel in the heart of fashionable Mayfair and at the centre of London's most exclusive shopping area. Originally American-owned, the hotel was opened in 1955 – the first luxury hotel to be built in London for a quarter of a century.

Hotels at Heathrow and Gatwick airports
All have maximum insulation against noise, 24-hour service and courtesy buses:

Ariel Hotel Bath Road, Hayes, Middlesex. Tel 759 2552

Excelsior Hotel Bath Road, West Drayton, Middlesex. Tel 759 6611

Post House Hotel Sipson Road, West Drayton, Middlesex. Tel 759 2323

Skyway Hotel Bath Road, Hayes, Middlesex. Tel 759 6311

Post House Hotel (Gatwick) Povey Cross Road, Horley, Sussex. Tel (02934) 71621

Trusthouse Forte Central Reservations Office
For world-wide reservations at any THF Hotel telephone 567 3444

Restaurants

In common with other large capital cities, London has a very wide choice of restaurants, ranging from luxury restaurants offering *haute cuisine* menus to cheaper Greek, Indian and Chinese establishments, as well as hamburger joints, health food restaurants and pizzerias. The more exclusive restaurants – usually French – are found (along with Italian) in Covent Garden, Piccadilly, Knightsbridge, Kensington and Chelsea. Chinese restaurants are in the Gerrard Street area of Soho, while Greek (more often Greek-Cypriot) places are congregated around Charlotte Street. Both Queensway and Hampstead offer concentrations of varied restaurants.

For some of the more popular and better known restaurants, it is advisable to book, especially for Friday and Saturday nights. Many are closed on Sundays.

English menus often require some mental arithmetic: cover charges, service charge, and VAT are sometimes included, sometimes not – most frequently, some permutation of the three is extra (and, due to a higher mark-up on wine than is usual in most other European countries, drinking with meals is always relatively expensive).

A choice of restaurants – divided into types of cuisine – is given below, with a rough indication of the price for a meal for two, including wine and extras.
£ = *c*.£15. ££ = *c*.£25. £££ = *c*.£40.

(THF) A Trusthouse Forte Restaurant

American

Hard Rock Cafe
150 Old Park Lane W1
Tel 629 1382 £

Probably necessary to queue for a table at this popular hamburger joint where they charcoal-grill to order. They also do steaks, salads and elaborate desserts in huge portions. Non-stop blaring rock music and drinks at the bar.

Joe Allen
13 Exeter Street WC2
Tel 836 0651 ££

Trendy, fashionable restaurant in a converted warehouse in Covent Garden with a blackboard menu of steaks and hamburgers and other 'American' dishes too, from Caesar salads to Eggs Benedict. Open till late. Also cocktails.

Julie's Pantry (THF)
52 Brompton Road SW3
Tel 584 6781 £

One of a small chain offering the best in the burger range, with smart modern decor. Rated top in a fast-food survey which gave it the accolade of serving the best doughnuts in Britain.

Peppermint Park
13-14 Upper St Martin's Lane WC2
Tel 836 5234. Open until 2am, Sun midnight ££

Brightly decorated in minty pinks and greens, this fashionable restaurant serves an exciting selection of cocktails and 'American' food, from hamburgers to hot dogs and salt beef. Very loud music makes conversation difficult.

Wolfe's of Park Lane
34 Park Lane W1
Tel 499 6899 £

A somewhat cramped but luxurious hamburger joint down the road from the Hilton with smart waitresses and ice-cream desserts. Posher than most, but typical American food.

Carveries & Steak Houses

Carvery Restaurants (THF) £

As the name suggests, the fixed-price menu in these popular restaurants includes a carve-yourself selection of excellent roast meats. Available at the *Cumberland Hotel* Marble Arch (262 1234); *Regent Palace Hotel* Piccadilly Circus (734 7000); *Hotel Russell* Russell Square (837 6470); *Strand Palace Hotel* Strand (836 8080) and the *City Yacht* London Wall (see below). Carvery restaurants are also to be found at the *Excelsior Hotel* (759 6611) and the *Post House Hotel* (759 2323) at London Heathrow Airport.

City Yacht (THF)
Addle Street EC2
Tel 606 8536. Lunch only, closed Sat & Sun ££

An exclusive rendezvous for City businessmen in the heart of the Barbican development. First-class *à la carte* selection and fine wines as well as good roasts in the Carvery.

Henekey's Steak Houses (THF) £

A grill-style menu at popular prices in traditional surroundings. In Argyll Street W1 (437 1143); Leicester Square WC2 (839 3622); *White Bear Inn* Piccadilly Circus SW1 (930 7901); Piccadilly W1 (437 9980); Jermyn Street SW1 (930 5339); Lawrence Lane EC2 (606 2373) and Ealing W5 (567 1336).

Chinese

Chuen-Cheng-Ku
17 Wardour Street W1
Tel 437 1398 ££

A maze of rooms that always seem to be full, and usually of Chinese. Interesting menu for the adventurous including: 'giant bowels', 'fried chicken blood', 'eels' and other delicacies. Other more familiar dishes are equally good.

Lee Ho Fook
15 Gerrard Street W1
Tel 734 9578
or 5-6 New College Parade, Finchley Road
NW3
Tel 722 9552 £
The older branch is in Gerrard Street, but
some say Finchley Road is better. Famous
for its *dim sum* (steamed savouries in a
bamboo basket), the fish is also good.

Poons
4 Leicester Street WC2
Tel 437 1528. Closed Sun £
or 41 King Street WC2
Tel 240 1743. Closed Sun ££
The Leicester Street branch (under separate
management) is just round the corner from
its more expensive namesake. Cantonese
cooking with the emphasis on wind-dried
meats. King Street has 350 different dishes
emerging from the kitchen, which is in full
view of customers.

Dutch

My Old Dutch
132 High Holborn WC1
Tel 242 5200
or 31 Dover Street W1
Tel 499 4316 £
Authentic Dutch pancake house that serves
huge pancakes on vast, original Delft plates.
Lots of varieties, savoury and sweet. Very
loud taped music and fast service.

English

George & Vulture (THF)
Castle Court EC3
Tel 626 9710. Lunch only, closed Sat &
Sun ££
Rebuilt after the Great Fire of London, this
is reputed to be the oldest tavern in the
world and is the favourite eating place of
City gentlemen. Charles Dickens wrote *The
Pickwick Papers* while staying here, and the
Dickensian atmosphere survives. Renowned
for thick chops and juicy steaks and its
'Pickwick' steak, kidney and mushroom
pudding.

Grange
39 King Street WC2
Tel 240 2939. Closed Sat & Sun lunch ££
Sophisticated restaurant with elegant decor.
Crisp white tablecloths, formal service and a
monthly-changing menu with a choice of
two- or four-course set meals. Mainly
English food, with some French.

Hunting Lodge (THF)
Lower Regent Street SW1
Tel 930 4222. Closed Sat lunch & Sun ££
Specialising in game and poultry, this
restaurant has a high reputation for
traditional English dishes like jugged hare
and steak and kidney pie. Comprehensive
wine list, with many fine Bordeaux reds.

Rules
35 Maiden Lane WC2
Tel 836 5314. Closed Sat lunch & Sun £££
One of the oldest eating houses in London,
serving solid English specialities in much the
same way it has been doing for 200 years.
Ask for a table downstairs.

Seasons Restaurant (THF)
289 Upper Regent Street W1
Tel 636 7006 £
Good, quick-service restaurant ideal for
shoppers. Coffee shop opens 8am.

Simpsons
100 Strand WC2
Tel 836 9112. Closed Sun ££
A traditional English restaurant noted for its
excellent meat. Roast beef, duck or saddle of
mutton from the trolley are always good.

Tate Gallery
Millbank SW1
Tel 834 6754. Lunch only, closed Sun ££
Not the sort of restaurant to be expected in
an art gallery but recognised as excellent,
serving enterprising English dishes and some
French. Excellent wine list.

Upper Crust
9 William Street SW1
Tel 235 8444 £
Sophisticated pie shop in Knightsbridge
with interesting fillings such as giblet and
pickled walnut, and pie puddings too. Also
roasts and boiled meats.

Fish

Geales'
2 Farmer Street W8
Tel 727 7969. Closed Sun & Mon £
Reasonably priced fish and chips in a 1930s
tearoom setting.

Le Suquet
104 Draycott Avenue SW3
Tel 581 1785. Closed Mon & Tue lunch
£££
A truly 'French' fish restaurant with a
serious attitude to fish in a busy but rather
informal atmosphere. Huge 'plateau de
fruits de mer' and shell-fish take-away.

Wheelers
19 Old Compton Street W1
Tel 437 7661 £££
This is the oldest (120 years) restaurant in a
large chain of seafood restaurants. Formal,
red plush setting and enormous portions,
with good Dover sole and shellfish.

French

Au Bon Accueil
27 Elyston Street SW3
Tel 589 3718. Closed Sun & Sat lunch ££
Excellent, reasonably priced French food
served in a small, unpretentious restaurant
with three inter-connecting rooms and a
cellar. Tables on the pavement in summer.

Carrier's

2 Camden Passage N1
Tel 226 5353. Closed Sun £££

In Camden Passage antiques market, an
intimate restaurant with simple decor but
sophisticated food. Set 4-course menu of
classic dishes, superbly presented.

Chez Solange

35 Cranbourn Street WC2
Tel 836 0542. Closed Sun £££

This busy French-owned restaurant has
been serving excellent classic French dishes
for over 20 years. Right next to Leicester
Square, they have a large menu that they
often change and an interesting wine list
covering lesser-known regions of France.

Daphne's

112 Draycott Avenue SW3
Tel 589 4257. Dinner only, closed Sun £££
A smart, classical French restaurant, with
plat du jour chalked up on a blackboard and a
short *table d'hôte* with unusual creations.

Langan's

Stratton Street W1
Tel 493 6437. Closed Sat lunch & Sun £££
A busy and fashionable brasserie with
seating for 200 people and live music every
night. The menu is varied and interesting.

Le Chef

41 Connaught Street W2
Tel 262 5945. Closed Sat lunch & Sun £££
Typical French bistro with red checked
tablecloths on two floors and taped Piaf
music. Simple, well-prepared dishes.

L'Etoile

30 Charlotte Street W1
Tel 636 1496 £££

Charming and reliable restaurant some 50
years old, offering unusual regional
specialities. Serious eating off starched
tablecloths. Attentive and formal waiters.

Leith's

92 Kensington Park Road W11
Tel 229 4481. Dinner only £££

A very 'personal' and smart establishment
with a fixed price menu of French-inspired
dishes and some 'nouvelle-cuisine' too.

Greek

Anemos

34 Charlotte Street W1
Tel 636 2289 or 580 5907. Closed Sun £££
Exceptionally jolly atmosphere in this fairly
typical Greek taverna, with waiters and
enthusiastic guests dancing on the tables.
Good food and loud Greek music.

Aphrodite

156a Seven Sisters Road N7
Tel 263 2047. Closed Sun £

Spacious, lively restaurant popular with the
Cypriot locals who use it for parties. Good
meze. Bouzouki group Wed-Sat from 9pm.

Beoty's

79 St Martin's Lane WC2
Tel 836 8768. Closed Sun £££

Elegant restaurant on two floors patronised
by publishers and politicians. Greek specialities. Quiet atmosphere, courteous service.

Elysée

13 Percy Street W1
Tel 636 4140 £££

Well-established and elegant restaurant with
traditional dishes: shashlik, kebab, etc.
Warms up after 9pm with bouzouki music
and dancing. Cabaret three times nightly.
Very good atmosphere: roof garden.

Kalamaras

66 or 76 Inverness Mews W2
Tel 727 5082 or 727 9122. Closed Sun £££
Two small and friendly Greek tavernas in a
mews behind Queensway serving authentic
Greek food. Bouzouki music on some
evenings. Restaurant at No 66 unlicensed.

Nontas

16 Camden High Street NW1
Tel 387 4579. Closed Sun £

Crowded and popular Greek Cypriot taverna
with attractive decor and recorded Greek
music. Candlelit tables, kebabs of meat,
chicken or fish and good crispy squid.

Health/Vegetarian

Cranks

In Heals at 196 Tottenham Court Road W1
Tel 637 2230. Open 10-5, closed Sun £
Airy restaurant on the 4th floor with a self
service counter of home-made soups, hot
savouries, salads and organic vegetables.
Tables shared by people who take eating
health food seriously but don't mind putting
on weight after their delicious puddings.

Food for Thought

31 Neal Street WC2
Tel 836 0239. Closed Sat & Sun £

Tiny vegetarian restaurant in Covent
Garden. Hot and cold savouries, quiches,
soups, salads. Self-service and 'take-away'.

Hungarian

Gay Hussar

2 Greek Street W1
Tel 437 0973. Closed Sun £££

Much loved and well established restaurant
just off Soho Square with a large menu of
Hungarian specialities and a friendly staff.

Indian

Last Days of the Raj

22 Drury Lane WC2
Tel 836 5705 ££

A new restaurant with eight owners from
India, Bangladesh and Nepal, all offering
interesting specialities. Try their tandoori
selection. Sweets include home-made
ice-cream. House wines are French bottled.

Standard Indian
21-23 Westbourne Grove W2
Tel 727 4818 or 229 0600 £
Unpretentious and very popular restaurant
on two floors with good 'nan' and tandoori
dishes and very reasonable prices.

Veeraswamy's
99-101 Regent Street W1
Tel 734 1401 ££
Rather formal club-like atmosphere with a
turbanned doorman and colonial-style decor.
Good food.

International

The Café Royal (THF)
Regent Street W1
Tel 437 9090 £££
World renowned for its cuisine, with the
luxurious *Le Relais* restaurant, the elegant
Grillroom, and 21 banqueting and conference
suites. In the past frequented by Oscar
Wilde, Bernard Shaw, Augustus John, Max
Beerbohm and many other celebrities. The
famous cellars stock some 150,000 bottles
including over 90 château-bottled clarets.

Jules' Bar (THF)
85 Jermyn Street SW1
Tel 930 4700. Lunch only, eve drinks,
closed Sun ££
Built originally as the *Waterloo Hotel* in 1830
and turned into a restaurant in 1903 by Jules
Ribstein. Renowned for wide selection of
cocktails, charcoal grills and cold buffet.

Serpentine Restaurant (THF) and
Pergola Restaurant (THF)
Hyde Park SW1
Tel 723 8784. Closed Sun lunch £
Attractive restaurants in park setting,
popular with visitors to London.

Tapas
30 Winchester Street SW1
Tel 828 3366. Closed Sun ££
Warm and intimate downstairs restaurant
with delicious dishes from all over the world,
and exceptional wine list.

Italian

Le Terrazza
19 Romilly Street W1
Tel 734 2504 ££
Elegant restaurant with spotlit tables and
potted plants. Serves good but predictable
Italian food at slightly above average prices.

Montpeliano
13 Montpelier Street SW7
Tel 589 0032. Closed Sun ££
Tightly packed tables with some on the roof
in summer, serving authentic Italian food.

Ristorante San Martino
46 St Martin's Lane WC2
Tel 240 2336 ££
A good three-course set menu, with
home-made pasta. Handy for theatreland.

San Frediano
62 Fulham Road SW3
Tel 584 8375. Closed Sun ££
Busy, bustling trattoria where they take both
customer and food seriously. Attractive cold
table and good food from the kitchen.

Jewish

Bloom's
90 Whitechapel High Street E1
Tel 247 6001. Closed Fri dinner & Sat ££
Enjoy the food but not necessarily the
service in this kosher restaurant in London's
East End. Long established with huge
portions and a bright and busy atmosphere.
Take-away salt beef sandwiches from the
counter.

Lebanese

Fakhreldine
85 Piccadilly W1
Tel 493 3426 ££
Over 40 different hors d'oeuvres are offered
in this luxury restaurant overlooking Green
Park. Charcoal grills with 'chef's own'
sauces.

Maroush
21 Edgware Road W2
Tel 262 9585 ££
Stylish new restaurant with traditional
Lebanese dishes cooked in a brick oven,
accompanied by delicious salads. Open until
dawn.

Scandinavian

Danish Coffee House
16 Sloane Street SW1
Tel 235 8521. Open 9-5, closed Sun £
Modern basement under the Danish Shop
and close to Knightsbridge shops. Danish
open-sandwiches from a counter which also
offers pastries, salads and good coffee. Also
handy for a quick cup of tea. Unlicensed.

The Hungry Viking
44 Ossington Street W2
Tel 727 3311. Closed lunch, Mon ££
As its name implies it's necessary to be
hungry to eat in this typically Scandinavian
restaurant which offers a huge self-service
smorgasbord (cold) table. A meal could
include soup, marinated herring, cold roast
meat, salads and pudding, with as many
helpings as desired.

Spanish

Martinez
25 Swallow Street W1
Tel 734 5006 ££
There aren't many authentic Spanish
restaurants in London but this is one, tucked
away between Regent Street and Piccadilly.
Old-fashioned with lovely tiles and Spanish
decor, the restaurant is approached by a
grand staircase. Guitarist on some evenings.

Wine Bars

For those who want to enjoy wine – on its own, or with reasonably priced food – London has a rapidly-growing range of wine bars for every palate and pocket. Connoisseurs, though, should not expect erudite or specialised wine lists, although there are sometimes surprise finds in the most modest bars.

Unless otherwise listed, wine bars have the same opening hours as pubs. In the City they usually close in the early evening, and at weekends. Telephone first to check, in case they have changed their arrangements.

Key to abbreviations:
B Breakfast L Lunch
D Dinner C Connoisseur
wine list

Archduke

Concert Hall Approach, South Bank SE1
Tel 928 9370. Mon-Fri LD. No L Sat, closed Sun
Imaginatively designed on three levels inside the arches of the old railway bridge, behind the Royal Festival Hall. Ideal for before or after concerts and theatre. Good snacks downstairs, restaurant upstairs (with live music). Well-chosen wine.

Bill Bentleys

31 Beauchamp Place SW3
Tel 589 5080. Mon-Sat LDC. Closed Sun
Lively bar with traditional panelled rooms and small patio. Renowned for fine oysters and fish. Not cheap. Other branches at 239 Baker Street W1 (Regent's Park) and at 202 Bishopsgate EC1.

Blakes'

32-34 Wellington Street WC2
Tel 836 5298. Every day LD
Extrovert, sometimes noisy, attracting a young crowd. Unique selection of 15 English savoury pies, as well as hot dishes, and wines at reasonable prices. Coffee and cakes in the afternoon.

Bow Wine Vaults

1 Bow Churchyard EC4
Tel 248 1121. Mon-Fri LC. Eves 5-7
Traditional decor, a favourite venue for City men. Good hot and cold buffet. Wide selection of French and German wines, fairly priced. Wine shop next door.

Bubbles

41 North Audley Street W1
Tel 734 7807. Mon-Sat LDC. Closed Sun
Under the same management as *The Cork and Bottle*, with a similar wine list and excellent cold buffet, this wine bar offers a perfect respite for West End shoppers.

Café de la Gare

19 York Road SE1 (by Waterloo Station)
Tel 928 9761. Mon-Fri BLD. 8am-midnight. Closed Sat & Sun
Charming version of a French cafe, with English or Continental breakfast served until 11am. Very good snack meals, omelettes or set menus with French dishes, and grills. Interesting French wine list.

Café St Pierre

29 Clerkenwell Green EC1
Tel 251 6606. Tube: Farringdon Road. Mon-Sat BLDC. No D Sun & Mon
Attractive oasis in off-beat area with Left-Bank decor. Restaurant upstairs, snacks (quiche etc.) downstairs. Popular for Sunday lunches. Fairly priced wines.

Coates'

45 London Wall EC2
Tel 628 5861. Mon-Fri LC. Eves 5-7
Splendidly traditional, full of City brokers and underwriters. An old-established place owned by an independent wine firm. Well-prepared English food, hot and cold. Excellent wine list and good port from the barrel. Another branch at 109 Old Broad Street EC2 (same hours).

Cork and Bottle

44-46 Cranbourn Street WC2
Tel 734 7807. Mon-Sat LDC. Closed Sun
In the heart of theatre and cinemaland. Extremely popular, with occasional live music. Beautifully displayed cold buffet. List of about 150 wines. Champagnes at very fair prices.

Daly's

46-48 Essex Street (210 Strand) WC2
Tel 583 4476. Mon-Fri BLD. Buffet only after 8pm. Bar closes 9.30 pm. Closed weekends.
Lawyers, journalists, bankers and publishers crowd into the spacious bar or eat downstairs in the restaurant. Edwardian atmosphere. Superb cheeses from the famous Paxton & Whitfield shop, good pates. Main menu features charcoal grills and French dishes. Sensible choice of wine. Open for breakfast from 8.30 am.

Davy's Wine Bars

(Information: Tel 858 6011)
From Covent Garden as far as Croydon, these old-style but modish wine bars – complete with sawdust on the floors – are owned by a family wine firm. Recommended are:

Mother Bunch's
Old Seacoal Lane (off Ludgate Hill) EC4
Tel 236 5317. Mon-Fri L eves 5.30-8.30
A popular venue for journalists and legal people, especially at lunchtime, with good port and sherry, well-selected wines and excellent cold table.

Gyngleboy
27 Spring Street W2
Tel 723 3351. Mon-Fri LD. Closed Sat & Sun
Within sprinting distance of Paddington Station, an unusual conversion of a former branch of Barclays Bank. Good snacks and cold food, and the reliable Davy wine list.

Draycott's
114 Draycott Avenue SW3
Tel 584 5359. Every day
LDC. No D Sat & Sun
In the fashionable
Chelsea-Knightsbridge
borders, with Edwardian
decor and a jolly, youngish
clientele. Interesting hot
and cold food. Above
average wine list.

Ebury
139 Ebury Street SW1
Tel 730 5447. Every day
LDC
Its advisable to book a table
at this popular wine bar with
its smart and attractive
buffet which also offers
good hot dishes. Excellent
wine list.

El Vino
47 Fleet Street EC4
Tel 353 6786. Mon-Fri LD
until 8. Sat L
Popular gossip shop for
(mainly male) journalists.

Fino's
12 North Row (nr Marble
Arch) W1
Tel 491 7261 Mon-Fri LD.
Closed Sat & Sun
One of a group of five in the
West End. Cosy, Victorian
style, on two floors. Noted
for roast beef, good snacks
and fairly priced wines. The
newest branch is in Swallow
Street W1 (by Piccadilly
Circus).

Gate Street
10 Gate Street WC2
Tel 404 0358. Mon-Fri LD.
Very convenient for
theatre-goers, cool modern
bar with original snacks
including a varied hot and
cold menu. Well compiled
wine list.

Genevieve Wine Bar
11 Thayer Street W1
(nr Wigmore Street)
Tel 486 2244. Mon-Fri
LDC. Open until midnight
Convenient for West End
shoppers, this elegant
ground floor bar shares the
exceptional wine list of its
parent (and more expensive)
restaurant above. Interesting
light dishes, good budget-
priced set meals.

Loose Box
136 Brompton Road SW3
(entrance also in Cheval
Place)
Tel 584 9280. Mon-Sat LD.
Closed Sun
Horsey decor, lots of bustle.
This wine bar attracts the
young Chelsea crowd,
visiting foreigners, Harrods
shoppers and buyers and
sellers from the nearby
Bonham's auction rooms.
Cold buffet is the best
choice. Large, reasonable
wine list.

Russkies
6 Wellington Terrace,
Bayswater Road W2
(opposite Kensington Palace
Gardens)
Tel 229 9128. Mon-Sat
LDC. Sun 7-10.30
Facing the Russian
Embassy, hence the name,
this small Victorian-style
bar is owned by a wine
merchant. It has an
excellent wine list (note the
Spanish section) and
well-prepared hot and cold
food.

Slatters'
3 Panton Street WC2
Tel 839 4649. Mon-Sat LD
(until midnight). Closed
Sun
In the heart of Theatreland.
Intimate and relaxed, with
classical background music.
Short list of hot and cold
food, well-chosen wines
(reduced price house wine
from 8-10).

Solanges'
11 St Martin's Court WC2
(off St Martin's Lane)
Tel 240 0245. Mon-Sat LD
Good place to eat before or
after the theatre. Informal
French cafe setting with
collection of original Art
Deco posters. Shares the
same good wine list
(interesting for
lesser-known French) as its
parent restaurant adjoining.
Very reasonably priced
meals and snacks.

Pubs

The English pub is a unique
institution, being as much a
social focus for its area – or
local trade – as it is a
drinking place. Although in
London many are on sites
which have housed pubs for
generations, a large number
have been rebuilt or
refurbished – often
destroying their character –
while others have been more
traditionally restored. Our
selection covers a wide range
in different areas, including
pubs which offer
entertainment.

Pubs are only open during
certain hours. In general,
these are 11am-3pm (parts
of the City, East End and
south of the river
10.30am-2.30pm) and
5.30-11pm. Sundays 12
noon-2pm & 7-10.30pm.
Most City pubs close at 8pm
and are closed on Sat & Sun.
Several central pubs close on
Sundays.

Food in pubs This ranges
from bar snacks to cold and
hot buffet or full meals.
Some pubs have separate
restaurants.

English Beer All pubs serve
both bottled and draught
beer. If you like it light and
cold, order the first,
specifying lager. Draught
beer, called bitter, is served
in half-pint and pint glasses.
Types of bitter vary
considerably, so if in doubt,
seek guidance from the bar.
Real ale – individual brews
of beer drawn through hand
pumps – is now more widely
available in pubs.

Free Houses Pubs not owned
by a particular brewery,
which offer a range of ales.

Albert
52 Victoria Street SW1
Tel 222 5577
Opulently Victorian. Starts
the day (unlike most pubs)
by serving delicious British
breakfasts from 8-11. Lunch
and dinner (Mon-Fri only)
are in the upstairs restaurant
and include good roasts.

Black Friar
174 Queen Victoria Street
EC4
Tel 236 5650   *Free House*
On the site of an old
Dominican priory, this
unique pub has an *art
nouveau* interior, with a
beaten bronze and copper
mural of friars at work. Bar
snacks only (lunchtime).

The Old Bull and Bush
North End Way,
Hampstead NW3
Tel 455 3638
An old farmhouse built in
1645, once the home of
William Hogarth, the pub
was made famous by the
Edwardian music hall song
'Down at the Old Bull and
Bush'. Always popular with
walkers on Hampstead
Heath. Good beer, bar
snacks and atmosphere.

Ye Olde Cheshire Cheese
Wine Office Court,
145 Fleet Street EC4
Tel 353 6170   *Free House*
Dating from the Great Fire,
this is one of London's most
famous pubs. Sawdust is
still strewn on the floor and
the atmosphere has
probably changed little since
Dr Johnson and his circle of
friends were 'regulars'. The
strong literary associations
include W. M. Thackeray,
Thomas Carlyle, Conan
Doyle, G. K. Chesterton
and W. B. Yeats.
Medium-priced restaurant
with notable pies and
puddings, especially 'Ye
Pudding' served in early Oct
and weighing 56 lbs.

Ye Olde Cock Tavern
22 Fleet Street EC4
Tel 353 3454
Originally further down the
street, this was a flourishing
inn in the 17th c. It closed
in 1665 because of the
plague, but had reopened by
1668 and was frequented at
various times by Samuel
Pepys, Dr Johnson and
Alfred Tennyson. It moved
in 1887 to its present site.
(The Dickens Room has
some of the original
furnishings.) Large dining
room (booking essential).

Dickens Inn by the Tower
St Katharine's Way,
St Katharine's Dock E1
Tel 481 1786   *Free House*
Most unusual converted
19th-c. warehouse in sight
of Tower Bridge,
overlooking yacht marina
and historic ship museum.
Seafood and snack bar,
terrace seating outside.

Dove Inn
19 Upper Mall, Chiswick
W6
Tel 748 5405
17th-c. riverside pub
patronised by J. M. W.
Turner who came here to
paint the Thames.
Congenial atmosphere,
especially in the evening.

Flask
77 Highgate West Hill N6
Tel 340 3969
A genuine 17th-c. building
of great charm, in the heart
of one of London's most
attractive 'villages'. The pub
was named after the flasks of
spring water sold here when
Hampstead was a spa in the
18th c. The highwayman
Dick Turpin is reputed to
have hidden in the cellars,
and they say William
Hogarth used to drink here.
Snacks and meals served in
the main bar. Big forecourt
with tables for open-air
drinking.

George Inn
Borough High Street,
Southwark SE1
Tel 407 2056
London's last remaining
galleried inn was built for
medieval pilgrims on their
way to Canterbury. It was
regularly patronised by
William Shakespeare who
lived in Southwark and 300
years later by Charles
Dickens, who mentions it in
Little Dorrit. The
Elizabethan tradition of
performing plays at the inn
has been revived recently
with shows in summer
(phone for dates).
Steak-house type restaurant
on the first floor and very
fine ground-floor bar with
real ale.

Grenadier
18 Wilton Row (off Wilton
Crescent) SW1
Tel 235 3074
In a picturesque mews, this
former mess for the Duke of
Wellington's officers is now
one of Belgravia's most
fashionable pubs, filled with
military memorabilia.

Henekey Pubs (THF)
This chain of pubs offering
excellent bar food includes
Bin 11 Wine Bar Leicester
Square WC2 (839 2412) and
The Cockney Pride Piccadilly
Circus WC2 (930 5339).

Jack Straw's Castle
North End Way NW3
Tel 435 8374
Mentioned by Dickens, this
popular Hampstead pub in
the shape of a castle stands
near the highest point in
London (437ft).

King's Head & Eight Bells
50 Cheyne Walk SW3
Tel 352 1820
In one of Chelsea's most
beautiful riverside streets,
this decorative
Victorian-style pub attracts
a cosmopolitan crowd and
the occasional celebrity,
notably at Sunday
lunch-time and on summer
evenings. Good cold buffet.

Lamb & Flag
33 Rose Street, Covent
Garden WC2
Tel 836 4108
Built in 1623, with lovely
old wooden-beamed bar.
John Dryden was attacked
here for writing satirical
verse about Louise de
Kerouaille, Charles II's
mistress. Noted for strong
ales and excellent snacks.

Nell of Old Drury
29 Catherine Street, Covent
Garden WC2
Tel 836 5328
Opposite the Theatre Royal,
this pub has always been
popular with musicians,
opera singers and
theatregoers. Its most
famous patron was Charles
II, who came here regularly
to meet his actress mistress
Nell Gwyn.

Prince Regent
71 Marylebone High Street
W1
Tel 935 2018
Comfortable pub with open
fireplace. Regency
memorabilia, period
cartoons and a 'Dickens
showcase'. Good restaurant
(weekdays only) with a fine
collection of antique cheese
dishes. Mainly English
food.

Prospect of Whitby
Wapping Wall E1
Tel 481 1095
Named after a sailing barge,
this is a traditional
watermen's tavern dating
from 1520. Once a centre of
ill-repute, smuggling and
cockfighting, it was also a
good place from which to
watch the execution of
pirates. Very atmospheric
and popular with visitors.

Red Lion
2 Duke of York Street W1
Tel 930 2030
Wonderfully preserved
Victorian interior with
engraved mirrors and
mahogany panelling. This
pub attracts locals and
visitors alike. On warm days
they overspill onto the
pavement outside. Hot and
cold snacks served in ample
portions. Reasonable prices.

St Stephen's Tavern
10 Bridge Street,
Westminster SW1
Tel 930 2541
This bustling old pub is the
local for Members of
Parliament and lobby
correspondents: a division
bell rings when MPs need to
rush back to vote. Very
'clubby' atmosphere, with
snack bar and restaurant
specialising in British fare.

Sherlock Holmes
10 Northumberland Avenue
WC2
Tel 930 2644
Every kind of Holmes'
memorabilia decorate this
unique pub. Upstairs, lunch
or dine beside the
glassed-off reconstruction of
Holmes' study. Traditional
English food.

Spaniards Inn
Hampstead Lane NW3
Tel 455 3276
Used by Keats and
Coleridge when they lived
nearby, also by Byron and
Shelley, this historic pub
was built *c*. 1630 by the toll
gate which the highwayman
Dick Turpin leapt across on
his horse when fleeing from
London. The inn appears as
The Spaniards Tea Gardens
in Dicken's *Pickwick
Papers*. Attractive garden,
Turpin's Room wine bar.

Trafalgar Tavern
Park Row, Greenwich SE10
Tel 858 2507
A wonderful pub located
near the Queen's House and
the great classical buildings
of Greenwich. The
restaurant is famous for its
whitebait.

MUSICAL PUBS

Nostalgic

Clarence
53 Whitehall SW1
Tel 930 4808
This 18th-c. house is
well-preserved with
gaslight, sawdust on the
floor and wooden pews to sit
on. From Monday to
Thursday there's a medieval
minstrel who sings by
candlelight. Seven Real Ales
are served.

Pindar of Wakefield
328 Gray's Inn Road WC1
Tel 837 7269
Specially devoted to
old-time music hall, usually
on Thursday, Friday and
Saturday evenings. On
Sundays an old-time dance
band plays. Snacks and
'basket meals' available.
There is considerable
demand for the shows and
advance bookings should be
made (Tel 722 5395).

Folk

Archway Tavern
1 Archway Road, Highgate
N19
Tel 272 2840
Folk music, especially Irish,
is played here every
evening, sometimes mixed
with Country and Pop.

Jack the Ripper
84 Commercial Street E1
Tel 247 2845
All the gruesome history of
the notorious murderer is
displayed in this typical East
End pub, where resident
bands play Country and
Western music, usually
twice a week. (Telephone to
confirm).

Modern

Hope and Anchor
207 Upper Street N1
Tel 359 4510
London's best Punk pub.
Exotic and ragged clientele,
bands nightly downstairs.

One Tun (Finch's)
58 Goodge Street W1
Tel 636 7149 *Free House*
Jolly pub patronised by
medical students from the
nearby Middlesex Hospital.
Dixieland band plays several
times a week. Buffet food
available.

THEATRE PUBS

King's Head
115 Upper Street N1
Tel 226 1916
Closed Sun
Late Victorian, full of
atmosphere. Theatre
(usually Mon-Sat) is at the
back of the bar, and can be
watched while eating or
drinking (lunch and
dinner).

The Spice of Life
Cambridge Circus WC2
Tel 437 7013
'Theatre at a price you can
afford' is £1 plus 25p
membership fee. Bar snacks
to accompany lunchtime or
evening shows upstairs.

For detailed information on
a widely-based selection of
pubs all over London,
contact: The Pub
Information Centre,
2 Caxton Street SW1.
Tel 222 3232

Nightlife

London's nightlife extends far beyond cinemas, theatres, concerts and an evening out in the pub. There are any number of 'clubs' where you can dine and dance, listen to jazz, have a flutter on the tables or 'bop' the night away. While some clubs are for members only, most offer temporary membership, but it's best to ring first. Casinos are strictly controlled by the Gaming Board and it's necessary to apply 48 hours in advance for membership. Buy the *Evening Standard* or *Time Out* to see what's on.

The list below is not comprehensive, merely suggestions of a few places that offer different types of nightlife.

Cabaret

London offers several venues for 5-course banquets with wine and entertainment. Bookings can be made at the London Tourist Board Information Centre, Victoria Station SW1 or direct. Tel 408 1001.

Beefeater-By-The-Tower
Ivory House, St Katharine's Dock E1
Pageantry and continuous entertainment.

The Caledonian
Hanover Street W1
Scottish cabaret.

Cockney Cabaret and Music Hall
18 Charing Cross Road WC2
Entertainment from the Edwardian music hall.

London Room
Parker Street, Drury Lane WC2
Cabaret and dancing.

Elizabethan Rooms
190 Queen's Gate SW7
Tel 584 6616
Medieval feast.

L'Hirondelle
Swallow Street W1
Tel 734 6666
Dazzling floor show with dinner and dancing.

Jazz

100 Club
100 Oxford Street W1
Tel 636 0933

The Canteen
4 Great Queen Street WC2
Tel 405 6598
Jazz restaurant with live 40's and 50's music including jazz, blues and swing.

Ronnie Scott's
47 Frith Street W1
Tel 439 0747

Pizza Express
10 Dean Street W1
Tel 437 9595

Pizza on the Park
11 Knightsbridge SW1
Tel 235 5550
Pizza restaurants with jazz from 9pm-midnight.

Rock and Pop

Bull and Gate
389 Kentish Town Road NW5
Pub with rock bands.

Camden Palace
1a Camden Road NW1
Tel 387 0428
Good disco and live bands. Large dance floor, several bars and restaurant. The current 'in' place.

Dingwalls
Camden Lock, Chalk Farm Road NW1
Tel 267 4967
Live bands play nightly in dimly-lit pub warehouse.

The Marquee
90 Wardour Street W1
Tel 437 6603
London's best known centre, opened 23 years ago with live rock music and dancing.

The Rock Garden
6-7 The Piazza
Covent Garden WC2
Tel 836 1929
Small restaurant on two floors and cramped cellar with live groups and packed dance floor.

The Venue
160-162 Victoria Street SW1
Tel 834 5500
A big place that seats 600 (American fast food). Good lively bands and semi-circular dance floor.

Discos

Discos go in and out of fashion faster than it takes to write a guidebook. Which are 'in'? Don't try Annabel's or Tramps unless with a member, but most other clubs will offer temporary membership. Here are a few:

Legends
29 Old Burlington Street W1
Tel 437 9933
Popular trendy disco based on New York's Studio 54.

Samanthas
3 New Burlington Street W1
Tel 734 5425
Large dance floor and lots of small, smoky rooms, popular with young people.

Maximus
14 Leicester Square WC2
Tel 734 4111
Shaped like a Roman forum with a tiny dance-floor frequented by the young and popular with tourists.

Stringfellows
16 Upper St Martin's Lane WC2
Tel 240 5534
One of the newest and smartest clubs in London, cool and elegant with an amazing lightshow just before 3am each morning.

Studio Valbonne
62 Kingly Street W1
Tel 439 7242
Cosmopolitan club for the over 25's, with Polynesian decor including waterfalls and pools.

Folk

Dingles Folk Club
Adams Arms, Conway Street W1
(Thur only)

Crypt Folk Club
St Martin-in-the Fields, Trafalgar Square WC2
(Sun only)

Cock Tavern Folk Club
27 Great Portland Street W1
(Thur only)

Three Horseshoes Folk Club
Heath Street Hampstead NW3

Theatres

Many of London's theatres were built in the 19th c. on the site of old playhouses, but a few still bear traces of an historic past, such as the *Drury Lane* which was patronised by Charles II in the 17th c. A few theatres opened in the 30's: the *Adelphi*, the *Cambridge* and the *Phoenix*, for example. Post-war theatres include the *Mermaid* (now rebuilt once again) and of course the *National Theatre* which opened in 1976 on the South Bank. London's newest theatre (and arts complex) is the *Barbican* which opened in 1982 and is the London home of the Royal Shakespeare Company. Theatre agents sell tickets (they add on their commission). Try Keith Prowse, Tel 836 2184. Alternatively go to or telephone the theatre box office. Details of current shows are in the *Evening Standard* or the weekly listings magazine *Time Out*. *The Times* publishes an Entertainment Guide Preview with the Friday paper. Some London theatres can be booked by quoting a personal credit card number. On the day of the performance, half-price tickets are available from the Leicester Square Ticket Booth (Mon-Sat, for matinee tickets 12-2, for evening tickets 2-6.30). See map on inside back cover for location of West End Theatres. Major London theatres include:

Adelphi
Strand WC2
Tel 836 7611

Albery
St Martin's Lane WC2
Tel 836 3876

Aldwych
The Aldwych WC2
Tel 836 5405

Ambassadors
West Street WC2
Tel 836 1171

Apollo
Shaftesbury Avenue W1
Tel 437 2663

Astoria
157 Charing Cross Road WC2
Tel 437 6564

Barbican Theatre
Barbican EC2
Tel 638 8891
Home of the Royal Shakespeare Company. The Barbican Theatre is of revolutionary design and seats 1160. The Pit is a studio theatre that seats 200. The company present both new plays and classics.

Cambridge
Earlham Street WC2
Tel 836 6056

Comedy
Panton Street SW1
Tel 930 2578

Criterion
Piccadilly Circus W1
Tel 930 3216

Duchess
Catherine Street WC2
Tel 836 8243

Duke of York's
St Martin's Lane WC2
Tel 836 5122

Fortune
Russell Street WC2
Tel 836 2238

Garrick
Charing Cross Road WC2
Tel 836 4601

Globe
Shaftesbury Avenue W1
Tel 437 1592

Haymarket
Haymarket SW1
Tel 930 9832

Her Majesty's
Haymarket SW1
Tel 930 6606

Lyric
Shaftesbury Avenue W1
Tel 437 3686

Lyric
King Street, Hammersmith W6
Tel 741 2311

Mayfair
Stratton Street W1
Tel 629 3036

Mermaid
Puddle Dock EC4
Tel 236 5568

National Theatre
South Bank SE1
Tel 928 2252
Opened in 1976. Three theatres – Olivier, Lyttleton and Cottisloe. New plays, classics and experimental plays performed by the National Theatre Company. Also exhibitions, restaurant and buffets open before and after performances. Live music in the foyer – jazz, folk, classical. All seats bookable, some tickets retained for sale on the day released at 10am.

New London
Drury Lane WC2
Tel 405 0072

Palace
Cambridge Circus W1
Tel 437 6834

Phoenix
Charing Cross Road WC2
Tel 836 2295

Piccadilly
Denman Street W1
Tel 437 4506

Prince Edward
Old Compton Street W1
Tel 437 6877

Prince of Wales
Coventry Street W1
Tel 930 8681

Queen's
Shaftesbury Avenue W1
Tel 734 1166

Royal Court
Sloane Square SW1
Tel 730 1745

Royalty
Portugal Street, Kingsway WC2
Tel 405 8004

St Martin's
Cambridge Circus, West Street WC2
Tel 836 1443

Savoy
Strand WC2
Tel 836 8888

Shaftesbury
Shaftesbury Avenue WC2
Tel 836 6596

Strand
Aldwych WC2
Tel 836 2660

Theatre Royal Drury Lane
WC2
Tel 836 9108

Vaudeville
Strand WC2
Tel 836 9988

Victoria Palace
Victoria Street SW1
Tel 834 1317

Whitehall
Whitehall SW1
Tel 930 6692

Wyndham's
Charing Cross Road WC2
Tel 836 3028

Variety Theatres

London Palladium
Argyll Street W1
Tel 437 7373
Much sought-after venue for foreign variety artists. Royal Command Performance takes place annually.

Players'
Villiers Street WC2
Tel 839 1134
Victorian music hall with cheerful audience participation. Membership only but available two days in advance.

Fringe, Alternative and Arts Theatres

There are many small theatre companies scattered all over London, finding homes anywhere from in pubs to converted warehouses. For some membership is necessary; this has to be taken out at least half an hour before the performance. There is a Fringe Box Office at the *Criterion Theatre* Piccadilly Circus W1 Tel 839 6987 open Mon-Thur 10-6, Fri-Sat 10-5. There are too many fringe theatres to list, but here is a selection:

Bush Theatre
Shepherd's Bush Green W12
Tel 743 3388

Cockpit Theatre
Gateforth Street,
Marylebone NW8
Tel 402 5081

Hampstead Theatre
Swiss Cottage Centre NW3
Tel 722 9301

ICA Theatre
The Mall SW1
Tel 930 6393

Riverside Studios
Crisp Road W6
Tel 748 3354

Round House
Chalk Farm Road NW1
Tel 267 2564

The Place
17 Duke's Road WC1
Tel 387 0161

Theatre Royal
Stratford E15
Tel 534 0310

Theatre Upstairs
(Royal Court Theatre)
Sloane Square SW1
Tel 730 2554

Warehouse
41 Earlham Street WC2
Tel 836 1071

Young Vic
66 The Cut EC1
Tel 928 6393

Open-air Theatres

George Inn
77 Borough High Street SE1
Tel 703 2917
Historic pub (the last galleried pub in London, dating from 1676) with Shakespearian plays performed in the courtyard from May to July (Sat afternoon).

Holland Park Court Theatre
Holland Park W8
Tel 633 1707
Open-air theatre in summer and opera in July.

Regent's Park Open Air Theatre
Inner Circle, Regent's Park NW1
Tel 486 2431
Mainly Shakespeare from May-Aug.

For *Children's Theatre* see p. 76; for *Theatres in Pubs* see p. 96

Opera and Ballet

Coliseum
St Martin's Lane WC2
Tel 836 3161
Large London theatre seating 2400. The home of the English National Opera, with a wide repertoire of classical and modern operas.

Covent Garden
Royal Opera House, Bow Street WC2
Tel 240 1066
Home of the Royal Ballet and Royal Opera Company, but international opera and ballet stars and conductors perform here too.

Sadler's Wells
Rosebery Avenue EC1
Tel 837 1672
Acts as host to well-known ballet, mime and opera companies from all over the world. The Royal Ballet Company started here.

The Place
17 Duke's Road WC1
Tel 387 0161
Home of the London Contemporary Dance Theatre.

Concert Halls

London's concert halls offer a wide range of music – orchestral, choral, chamber and solo recitals plus jazz and light entertainment. Several London churches have lunchtime concerts on weekdays at midday, others have special concerts and music services with excellent choirs and organ recitals. For details of these contact the City Information Centre, St Paul's Churchyard, Tel 606 3030. In the summer months there are concerts in the open-air in several London parks, particularly on Sunday afternoons and during lunchtime. Information on South Bank Concert Halls, Tel 928 3002; ticket reservations Tel 928 3191.

Barbican Centre
Silk Street, Barbican EC2
Tel 628 8795
The *Barbican* is the home of the London Symphony Orchestra which performs three 4-week seasons (Mar, Jun-Jul & Nov). At other times the Barbican Hall, which seats 2000, holds many other forms of musical entertainment from recitals to 'pop' concerts.

Purcell Room
South Bank SE1
Chamber music and solo
performances in intimate
surroundings.

Queen Elizabeth Hall
South Bank SE1
Concerts by symphony
orchestras and bands plus
special poetry evenings and
music festivals.

Royal Albert Hall
Kensington Gore SW7
Tel 589 8212
Victorian domed hall built
in 1871. A variety of
different concerts including
classical, pop and choral and
the home of the Henry
Wood Promenade concerts.

Royal Festival Hall
South Bank SE1
Seats 3000 for orchestral and
choral concerts.

St John's Church
Smith Square SW1
Tel 222 1061
Lunchtime and evening
concerts, recitals and
chamber music in the
18th-c. church.

Wigmore Hall
38 Wigmore Street W1
Tel 935 2141
Fine acoustics in attractive
Edwardian hall. Chamber
music, recitals, instrumental
and song.

Cinemas

There are many different
kinds of cinema in London,
from private cinema clubs to
new cinema complexes
where there are three or four
small screens under one roof
showing the newest film
releases. Films are graded
by the British Board of Film
Censors. '18' means only
people over 18yrs will be
admitted; '15': 15yrs and
over; 'PG': parental
guidance (some scenes may
be unsuitable for children;
U: suitable for all ages.
Programmes are advertised
in the national press and
magazines like *Time Out* and
What's On. Cinemas open in
the afternoon and have two
or three different
performances. The Late

Night Film is often different
from the film shown in the
daytime. For reviews of new
releases look in the Sunday
papers and for descriptions
of current films see *Time
Out*.

West End Cinemas
These cinemas, specialising
in general releases, are
mainly around Leicester
Square and Piccadilly Circus
(see map on inside back
cover and daily press for
Tel Nos).

ABC
Shaftesbury Avenue W1
(1&2)

Carlton
Haymarket SW1

Cinecenta
Panton Street SW1 (1, 2, 3
& 4)
Piccadilly W1 (1, 2, & 3)

Classic
Haymarket W1, Charing
Cross Road WC2, Oxford
Street W1, Tottenham
Court Road W1

Columbia
Shaftesbury Avenue W1

Dominion
Tottenham Court Road W1

Empire
Leicester Square WC2
(1&2)

Film Centa
Charing Cross Road WC2
(1, 2, & 3)

Leicester Square Theatre
Leicester Square WC2

Odeon
Haymarket W1, Leicester
Square WC2, Marble Arch
W1

Plaza
Lower Regent Street W1 (1,
2, 3 & 4)

Prince Charles
Leicester Square WC2

Scene
Leicester Square WC2 (1, 2,
3 & 4)

Studio
Oxford Circus W1 (1, 2, 3 &
4)

Warner West End
Leicester Square WC2 (1, 2,
3, 4 & 5)

**Specialist and Membership
Cinemas**
Foreign films (usually
sub-titled) and films of
special artistic merit can be
seen in the West End and
other areas. Membership,
where it applies, can usually
be obtained at the door.

Academy
Oxford Street W1 (1, 2 & 3)

Barbican Centre
Silk Street EC2
Tel 628 8795
London's newest arts and
entertainment centre has a
public cinema with a
monthly season of films.

Camden Plaza
211 Camden High Street
NW1

Curzon
Curzon Street W1

Electric Cinema Club
191 Portobello Road W11

Everyman
Hampstead NW3

Gate Cinema Notting Hill
Notting Hill Gate W11

Gate Bloomsbury
Brunswick Square WC1

Gate Mayfair
Mayfair Hotel, Stratton
Street W1

ICA Cinema
Nash House, The Mall SW1

Lumiere
St Martin's Lane WC2

Minema
45 Knightsbridge SW1

National Film Theatre
South Bank SE1
Tel 928 3232
Seasons of special films
covering the work of a
particular actor or director.
Temporary membership is
available

Paris Pullman
Drayton Gardens SW10

Scala
Kings Cross N1

Screen on the Green
Islington Green N1

Screen on the Hill
230 Haverstock Hill NW3

Excursions

Chiswick GL B2

British Rail: Chiswick. Tube: Stamford Brook.
Bus: 27, 91, 237, 267, 290, E3.

Once a village outside London, Chiswick has now been swallowed up by suburbia, but **The Mall** along the river still has much of its village charm. In addition to the 18th c. terrace houses are two of London's finest historic inns, *The Dove* and *The Old Ship*, both particularly pleasant in the evening. Chiswick has always been popular with artists, and William Morris lived at *Kelmscott House* in the Mall. More recently the acting family of the Redgraves lived in Bedford House. In the parish **Church of St Nicholas** (rebuilt 19th c.) in Church Street at the W end of the Mall are buried William Kent (d.1764), who shared in the building of Chiswick House and Kensington Palace and built the Horse Guards, and the Anglo-American Impressionist James McNeill Whistler (d.1903).

W of the church and beyond the Chiswick (or Hogarth) Roundabout is **Hogarth's House** (p. 64), which was the artist's summer home for 30 years. Inside the lovely house are engravings of many of his best-known satirical works. A short walk further W leads on to **Chiswick House** (p. 43), a classical Italian masterpiece, built in 1729 by Lord Burlington as a 'temple of arts'.

Greenwich GL D2

British Rail: Greenwich, Maze Hill. River: from Charing Cross, Westminster or Tower pier. Tube: Surrey Docks then bus 10B, 188. Bus: 53, 54, 75, 177, 180, 185

With all its major attractions spread around a large park with commanding views, Greenwich makes a wonderful day's trip from the congestion of central London. The best way to travel is the route used by monarchs when they went to Greenwich: down the river. The boats disembark at Greenwich Pier, from where the complicated rigging of the **Cutty Sark** (p. 76) can be seen. Launched in 1869, it was the last of the tea-clippers. Beside it is *Gypsy Moth IV* in which Sir Francis Chichester sailed single-handed around the world.

¼m S, down Greenwich Church Street, is *St Alfege's Church*, whose patron martyr was stoned to death here by the Danes in 1011. Always an important church, Samuel Pepys liked it for 'a good sermon, a fine church and a great company of women'. The present building was designed by Nicholas Hawksmoor in 1712 (restored after war-time bomb damage) and contains one of the finest organs in England, played by Thomas Tallis – the father of English church music – between 1530-1585.

The best way to view Greenwich is from the *Isle of Dogs* on the N bank of the river (reached by a pedestrian tunnel), from where you can see the formal arrangement of buildings exactly as they were in the 18th c. when they were painted by Canaletto. The buildings nearest the river, in two wings, comprise the **Royal Naval College** (p. 56), built successively by four architects: Webb, Wren, Vanbrugh and Hawksmoor.

Centrally placed between the college and commanding an unbroken vista to the Thames is **The Queen's House** (p. 55), the first Palladian building in England, designed in 1616 by Inigo Jones and possibly the model for the American White House. On either side, connected by colonnades, are the wings of the **National Maritime Museum** (p. 67), which exhibits naval history.

On top of Greenwich Hill, in the Park, is the red-brick **Royal Observatory** (p. 67), designed by Sir Christopher Wren. The home of the Astronomer Royal from 1675 to 1948 (when pollution forced a move to Sussex), it is now part of the National Maritime Museum and houses a planetarium and collections showing the history of astronomy. The *Prime Meridian of Longitude* passes through it and a brass strip outside marks the division between E and W.

On the W edge of the Park (Chesterfield Walk) is the **Ranger's House** (p. 55), a 17th c. mansion enlarged in 1748 with a very fine collection of portraits. South of the Park is *Blackheath* (p. 74), a large open park once the haunt of highwaymen and footpads, now the centre of a prosperous residential area surrounded by Georgian terraces. On the river, just E of the Royal Naval College, is the historic *Trafalgar Tavern* (1837), celebrated for its whitebait dinners.

Hampton Court GL A3

British Rail: Hampton Court. River: from Westminster pier (summer only). Bus: 111, 131, 211, 216, 267, MV7, Green Line 715, 718, 725, 726

For 200 years the kings and queens of England and their visitors travelled up-river from Westminster to their favourite royal palace at Hampton Court.

Hampton Court Palace (p. 49, for the park p. 73) is the finest royal palace open to the public, a vast Tudor and 17th-18th-c. building with sumptuous state apartments and beautiful gardens. Separated by Hampton Court Road from the 'Home Park' is **Bushy Park** (p. 73). This was also part of the royal estate and still has deer roaming around in it. In the Chestnut Avenue, planted by Sir Christopher Wren and running S to the Palace, is the park's most famous feature, the *Diana Fountain* (1659).

The riverside *Mitre Hotel* opposite the palace serves good meals, and there are good restaurants and antique shops on the S side of the bridge and in Bridge Road.

Kew　　　　　　　　　　GL B2

British Rail: Kew Bridge. Tube: Kew Gardens.
River: from Westminster Pier (summer only).
Bus: 7, 27, 65, 90B

South of the river is *Kew Green*, once a
pleasant Georgian village green, now rather
spoilt by the road traffic. The parish *Church
of St Anne* (1714 with 1770 and 19th-c.
additions) has a mausoleum to the Dukes
and Duchesses of Cambridge who lived in
Cambridge House on the Green (now a wood
museum and part of the Royal Botanical
Gardens). W of the Green is the main
entrance to the **Royal Botanic Gardens**
(p. 75), matched nowhere in the world for
their combination of beauty and botanical
interest. Always lovely, the gardens are at
their peak in the spring. Within the gardens,
in addition to the temples, glasshouses,
pagoda and lake is the small **Kew Palace** or
Dutch House (p. 52) where King George III
lived.

On the N side of the Thames, on Kew
Bridge Road, is the **Kew Bridge Engines
Museum** (p. 65) where giant beam engines –
dating back to 1820 – can be seen operating
under steam. ½m further **W** is **Syon Park**
(house p. 57, park p. 75), with grounds laid
out by Capability Brown and a classical
mansion designed by Robert Adam.

Richmond　　　　　　　　GL B3

British Rail: Richmond. Tube: Richmond. River:
from Westminster Pier (summer only). Bus: 27,
33, 37, 72, 73, 90, 90B, 202, 270, 290

Once an independent town, Richmond is
now a prosperous suburb with good shops,
pubs and restaurants. NW of the station is
the *Old Deer Park* in which Henry VII's
royal palace once stood. Nothing remains
but the (heavily restored) *gatehouse* off the
17th c. *Richmond Green*. The walk down to
Richmond Bridge (built 1777) is very
pleasant and the towpath upstream (on the
W side) is one of the most attractive stretches
in London. It leads to **Marble Hill** (p. 53), a
perfect 18th-c. mansion built for King
George II's mistress. Just beyond it is the
Octagon, all that remains of *Orleans House*,
once the home of the exiled French Royal
Family. The Octagon was designed in 1720
by James Gibbs. Built onto it is a gallery
which often shows small exhibitions.

From opposite Marble Hill an erratic ferry
crosses the river (summer only) to **Ham
House** (p. 49). The house belonged to the
Duke of Lauderdale, whose fortune was
made when he became one of Charles II's
ministers in the famous 'Cabal'. It is an
outstanding mid 17th-c. brick house with
most of its original furniture still in place.
From Ham, a ½m walk down Ham Street
and Sandy Lane leads to the 2500 acres of
Richmond Park (p. 74), once royal hunting
grounds, now a public park with deer still
roaming free as they did in the Middle Ages.